Embracing
Elderhood

Planning for the Next Stage of Life

LAURIE L. MENZIES, ESQ.

Embracing Elderhood: *Planning for the Next Stage of Life*

For information about special discounts for bulk purchases, please contact the publisher.

Embracing Elderhood Press
1745 Hopkins Rd.
Getzville, NY 14068
716-204-1081

EmbracingElderhood.com
Laurie@EmbracingElderhood.com

First paperback edition November 2014

Embracing Elderhood can bring the author to your live event. For more information or to book an event, contact Embracing Elderhood at 716-204-1081 or visit our website at EmbracingElderhood.com

Designed by Jamie Baylis
JamieBaylis.com

Manufactured in the United States

Library of Congress control number 2014916795

ISBN: 978-0-9906497-0-0 (paperback)
         978-0-9906497-1-7 (ebook)

For My Mom and Dad

While he was in his nineties, my dad wrote in a book to me, called *A Father's Legacy*. In it, there was a question, "What word best describes your life?" His answer: "Happy. We were happy to be together."

That simple truth from my father is one of my greatest blessings. It is also the reason I can write this book with so much passion and love.

I hope everyone can feel that way someday.

CONTENTS

FOREWORD

ACED WITH THE OVERWHELMING and formidable task of living three full-time roles—caregiver for her aging and rapidly declining parents, spouse to her new husband, and partner in a growing elder law practice—Laurie Menzies experienced, firsthand, the issues on which she had been lecturing and counseling thousands of clients during her entire legal career. With the help of her husband, David, many friends, and her Higher Power, Laurie met the challenge. She successfully managed all three roles while maintaining an inner peace that filled her with joy in the most difficult and demanding stops in her journey with her mom and dad to heaven's gate.

Embracing Elderhood is the natural outgrowth of Laurie's personal experiences. She shares her journey of shepherding her mom and dad through their "elderhood," first by struggling on her own and then with the assistance of some of the many government benefits available to families faced with the dilemma of 24/7 care, limited resources, and limited time. This assistance came from local, state, and national programs designed to address the rapidly growing problems associated with aging.

Embracing Elderhood does not provide answers to the crisis of aging—instead, it offers options that are available both to the families with the foresight to plan, as well as to those who made no plans. Laurie shows that it is never too late to plan when it comes to elderhood and aging. Her legal, practical, and spiritual approach must not be missed.

In this book, Laurie shares her experience, strength, and hope with every family that finds itself faced with the challenges of aging in America. It is our hope that Laurie's story, told in layman's terms, will simplify your strategy and enable you to devote more time to loving your spouse, mom, or dad, and discover the beauty of this stage of life. This book can show you the way. We hope you find it helpful and useful as your journey begins.

— *Charles W. Beinhauer, Esq.*
Partner at Pfalzgraf, Beinhauer & Menzies
October 2014

PREFACE

CCORDING TO STATISTICS and the evidence all around us, we are going to live longer than we plan. Unfortunately, the longer we live, the more likely it is that some long-term care support will be needed. In its current state, the long-term care system is confusing, complex, and uncoordinated. Accessing services offered by the system often makes the difficult process of caring for aging loved ones harder than it should be.

A comprehensive approach is necessary to develop a plan for "elderhood." Some people call it *elder planning* or *long-term care planning* or even *estate planning*. Whatever we call it, the plan must consider the legal, financial, and care-management needs of an individual through the end of his or her life. Most seniors and their caregivers do not have a clear picture of how their finances will be managed when they need to pay for long-term care. Furthermore, they do not have a clear understanding of the progression of care, or where and how it can be accessed.

As the most recent commission tasked to report on the status of long-term care said:

> ... the network of providers [that] deliver support is complex, multifaceted, specialized, isolated from other service providers, and confusing to the average consumer.... Currently, there is no comprehensive approach to care coordination for these individuals and caregivers ...

Furthermore:

> Few providers ... evaluate a person's overall situation in order to arrange for the right combination of services based on one's actual needs. Instead, access to services is often organized in relationship to their funding streams, governed by a mix of federal, state, and local rules and procedures. Separate agencies may have unique eligibility rules, intake and assessment processes.
>
> — Commission on Long-Term Care,
> Report to the Congress, September 30, 2013

Every day I encounter families that are underinformed and underserved by the current long-term care system. Housing and health-care options for older individuals are determined, in large part, by finances. Unfortunately, many seniors receive inadequate long-term care because of misinformation regarding their money and the resources that could be available to them.

Coordinated advice can help families through the process of finding and paying for appropriate care for their loved ones. For example, a financial consultant would review and perhaps consolidate financial resources. Knowing what monies are available, a geriatric-care manager could then develop a care plan. Then, an elder law attorney could create a plan to reorganize the assets. This may enable the family to access government programs immediately or when they may be needed.

Long-term care plans involve many moving parts and require communication among the advisers and caregivers. Today most professionals do not engage in this type of coordinated planning. The system is not set up for professionals to get paid to work together. They still seem to be stuck in their silos, discussing only their particular products or services.

Today's system for long-term care is complicated, confusing, and disjointed. However, with help, we can make it work. We have to—for our families and ourselves. This book is written as honestly and clearly as possible, to serve as a starting point to help you understand how the pieces fit together.

Embracing Elderhood takes you through the same process I use when a client comes to me for advice. First, we have to know what the planning process is about. What is estate planning? How does it relate to long-term care issues? How much money are you bringing to the table? What do you expect to do with it? What will the care system look like when you have to access it? What are the various sources of payment available when care is needed? These are the questions that will be answered in the pages of this book.

As an elder law attorney who has been practicing in this area for 15 years, I have to admit that I was not prepared for the time, commitment, and advocacy required to effectively manage my parents' care through the end of their lives. Having successfully made it to the "other side," I am able to share some of the challenges we faced and mistakes we made along the way. The problem with being an exhausted child of aging parents is that, as much as you may want your old life back, it will never come. When you are finally finished with the job of caregiving for your loved ones, they are gone. You may forever rethink whether you did it right or what you could have done differently, but if you did it with love and with as much help and advice as you could get, you should have no regrets. I will always consider the time I spent helping my parents through their last years to be one of my greatest blessings.

I hope you find some new and useful information. I hope this book encourages you to work with a professional who has a caring and comprehensive approach. Finally, I hope you are excited to make a plan and enjoy elderhood—yours or that of your loved ones—together.

— *Laurie Menzies*
October 2014

I have used some of my father's cartoons throughout this book. When he could no longer walk independently and was home with my mom and his aides, he would sit at the table in the afternoon and write a comic strip. Starting at the age of 93, he created a comic every day for about a year and a half. While he always shared his great sense of humor, my father was a postal worker and volunteer fireman, not a cartoonist. When others may have focused on their disabilities, he found a hidden talent and used it to make other people happy. I have created a book of his drawings, called Young at Heart.

1

Embracing Elderhood

Y PARENTS ENJOYED their elderhood without running out of money. We pulled it off mostly because they didn't need help until my dad was 93. He lived 33 years longer than his dad. My mom lived 15 years longer than her mom. They were blessed to spend most of those extra years together, living independently and in good health.

As we enjoyed this time together, I didn't know there was a term for those extra years that I was able to enjoy with them. Now I realize that a lot of families are going to experience the same thing. In most cases, advances in health care and personal wellness have extended the life expectancies of most Americans well beyond the years for which they have planned. Most people know they should plan for retirement. Everyone knows they have to plan for what will happen when they die. But now we find ourselves with a "longevity bonus"—the years between ages 80 and 95 (or older)—that we will refer to as "elderhood."

When Mom and Dad needed me, I responded, and I saw myself in them. I see myself in the older people with whom I work. They tell me their fears and I realize they are the same as mine. In these moments of recognition, we remember that we are not alone. We are all in this thing called life together. When we help each other, we somehow know we are also helping ourselves.

Is it possible to embrace something that most of us don't even want to look at?

"Elderhood" is the term I have chosen to describe the stage of life that comes after adulthood. Current demographics indicate there are more of us experiencing elderhood than ever before. Given the constant advancements in medicine and technology, this trend will continue well beyond the foreseeable future.

The years we spend in our eighties and nineties can be either something to look forward to or something to fear. Unfortunately, most of us would rather not think about it. As a result, most people don't sufficiently plan for these years (and in many cases, don't plan at all). They experience them by default. This forces their children or the long-term care system to make decisions for them. It is no way to finish an otherwise good life. My heart breaks every time I pass a lonely face lined up against the wall in a nursing facility. How is it that he or she arrived at this point? I do not believe we have to accept this fate as inevitable.

ELDERHOOD		
Active Retirement *65 to 80*	Longevity Bonus *80 to 95+*	*Estate Plan* *(implemented at death)*

If the current system wasn't so expensive, complicated, and impersonal, we might not have so much fear. From my own life experience, fear is spawned from an absence of love.

Perhaps we can find a way to embrace this portion of our life's journey and make it better for those experiencing their elderhood. This will also help those of us who will be there sooner than we care to admit. If everyone involved with the long-term care system put enough love and practical effort into it, I know there would be a different outcome.

By definition, "embracing" something implies that we are accepting it or even welcoming it. To say that our society currently embraces elderhood would be a stretch. However, if we understand that the passage of time is inevitable, we can then accept that the odds favor the majority of us participating in this stage of life. This understanding paves the way for us to change the way we see elderhood and ultimately encourages us to plan for it.

I will be the first to admit that our current long-term care system is profoundly flawed. That is why I have written this book.

We must first become educated in the workings of our system as it currently exists. This book will lead you through everything you need to know to plan for a successful elderhood. Then, by working together, we can make better plans for the way we would like ourselves and our families to experience this precious time of life. By understanding our own particular financial and social situations, we can plan for the best experience possible.

Some people are thrown into the long-term care system quickly and violently—usually as the result of a sudden, catastrophic physical event, like a stroke or a broken hip. One bad fall for an older person can bring about a swift and dramatic change in his entire life situation. No wonder we fear growing old. It shows up uninvited. There are no social rituals or signposts announcing your arrival at elderhood. One day you are just there.

One bad fall for an older person can bring about a swift and dramatic change in his entire life situation.

Furthermore, there aren't many guidebooks available to help us plan for the experience of living past our 80th year, especially if we need assistance. The long-term care system is large, unwieldy, and impersonal. However, with knowledge and guidance, we can make the best of what it has to offer. If we would recognize that this is our future as well, we can work together to make it better. We have a stake in making it something we can all embrace.

We all fear the unknown. Most of the fear we have about aging is related to the reality that getting old often includes social, mental, and physical decline. But there is an upside to growing old. For one thing, it is better than the alternative. However, there is also the wisdom from our experience of the life that came beforehand. We can use this as a rubric for how we would like to finish the journey.

I believe that, through planning, we can alleviate many of the fears that surround our shared future. I would like to think that I can help change the way we understand and help each other through our old age. We can work together to create an elderhood that looks like something each of us will happily embrace in our own unique way.

2

WHAT IS
ESTATE PLANNING?

OR A LOT OF PEOPLE, their estate plan begins and ends with the signing of a last will and testament. The best thing about a basic will is it requires you to at least think about who would get what if you died soon with what you have now. It is a place to start, but not a plan. Estate planning is more than writing a will. It is really the process of:

- determining what you own
- determining what you want to happen to that property in the event of your incapacity or at death
- implementing that plan through legal documents and other asset transfer techniques.

Estate planning is difficult. You will have to discuss scenarios in which you are no longer in control of your assets. You are either incapacitated or have passed on.

Most people spend their lifetime growing and guarding their wealth. Understandably, we have a deep personal commitment to its preservation. We may not admit it, but our sense of security may be tied to the access and control of our assets.

Estate planning can also be stressful because it is complex. Creating and implementing a good estate plan should include at least three professional advisers: your financial adviser, your accountant, and an attorney who focuses his or her practice in this area. You should consider bringing together the key players you expect to be involved in your plan. This will ensure everyone is on the same page and prepared for his or her role, as needed, in the future.

If you don't plan for the time between retirement and death, the assets you have accumulated over your life may not be there for your heirs. Most people don't know enough about the long-term care services, supports, and the ways in which they will be paid. Planning for these potential needs can prevent unnecessary loss of wealth and alleviate future family stress. Not surprisingly, putting a plan in place for aging actually reduces stress. By asking the right questions, experienced advisers can help clients make decisions and design the life they want to live as they age.

Careful and prudent planning can significantly reduce unnecessary taxes and care costs. Just as important, it can replace potential family conflicts and stress with peace of mind.

The Role of Asset Ownership

The process of estate planning involves the preparation of certain legal documents and the adoption of one or more transfer

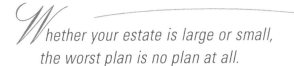

*hether your estate is large or small,
the worst plan is no plan at all.*

strategies for the remainder of your life and at death. These strategies are designed to allow your assets to pass to your intended beneficiaries in the most efficient manner.

The first thing you need to know about estate planning is what is in your estate. This begins by determining, in legal terms, who owns what. You have to review the title (ownership) of each of your assets. This is extremely important and yet so often misunderstood or not completely reviewed. When you buy a mutual fund, purchase a home, or open a bank account, the way you title the asset affects not only your immediate rights, but also how, and to whom, the asset will transfer upon your death.

I am constantly amazed at how many people truly don't know what they own. For example, if you own an account jointly with your husband, it is not "your" account just because your Social Security income is directly deposited into it. It is still a joint account for legal purposes.

An effective estate plan requires that ownership and beneficiary-designation documents be consistent with the plan. Far too often, these documents are inconsistent with a person's will, trust, or overall plan objectives. For instance, you cannot own a home jointly with one person and leave that same home to someone else in your will. Similarly, you cannot designate one person as a beneficiary under a life insurance policy and be certain that

IT MATTERS HOW YOU TITLE YOUR ASSETS

	Your assets are titled	What happens to your assets	Avoids probate
WHEN YOU USE A **WILL** . . .	SOLE OWNERSHIP In your name alone, e.g., "John Smith"	Pass via the terms of your will (without a will, sole ownership assets transfer via intestacy)	No
WHEN YOU USE **WILL SUBSTITUTES** SUCH AS . . .	JOINT (two types): • **Joint Tenant With Rights of Survivorship** *OR*	Pass to the survivor at death	Yes
	• **Joint Tenants in Common**	- Half goes to survivor - Half goes to your estate (probate)	No
	BENEFICIARY DESIGNATION: • **IRA** • **401(k)** • **annuity** • **life insurance** • **payable on death** • **transfer on death**	- Goes directly to name beneficiary at death - This designation overrides the terms of a will	Yes
	TRUST • **Revocable (Living Trust)**	Trustee (can be you) owns assets; at death, assets are distributed via terms of the trust	Yes
	• **Irrevocable**	Assets are removed from your ownership and control; you can receive income; can help protect your assets	Yes
	DEED TRANSFER WITH RETAINED LIFE ESTATE	Allows you to give the future ownership of your real property to others while maintaining current rights and obligations, such as residing at the property and tax exemptions	Yes

he or she will share with siblings or use the insurance proceeds to pay off your debts or funeral expenses.

If you haven't reviewed your assets to consider how they are titled (i.e., joint or individual) or whom you have named as the account beneficiary (e.g., on your annuity contract), you may be surprised to find out how your property would be distributed upon your death. Many assets have built-in transfer mechanisms such as rights of survivorship or beneficiary designations. Assets titled in your name alone will transfer according to the terms of your will, or via *intestacy* if no will exists.

Your will is only the outline of your intentions for the distribution of your wealth when you die. The real issues that you may be concerned with will likely involve the management and use of those assets during the remainder of your life. In most cases, you will not die with the exact asset structure that you have in place when you sign your will. Furthermore, your executor will not have any authority to act until you have died. A lot can (and probably will) happen to you and your money before that time.

I have a client who owned joint checking and savings accounts with his wife. He then purchased four separate certificates of deposit (CDs) at the bank, each designated to transfer-on-death to each of his four children. The accounts were owned jointly with his wife, so the kids wouldn't get them until they both passed away. This is a good idea if his only objective is to avoid probate. Looking ahead, which CD should we use first to pay for his care should he need it? The child he likes the least? Should we take a little out of each account?

If you would like to avoid *probate,* you need to know that your will controls the transfer of assets owned in your name alone, as well as those assets that do not have a built-in transfer mechanism such as *rights of survivorship* or *beneficiary designations.* For those assets, your will determines the distribution. Probate is the necessary process of proving the validity of your last will. It governs the procedures used by your executor to complete the collection and distribution of those assets that pass by the terms of your will. The court becomes involved because you are no longer here to speak for yourself.

In short, the court wants to ensure that your directions are followed. If you want to avoid probate, there are many other ways to ensure the proper distribution of your assets after you die.

Single ownership *(or sole ownership):* Asset ownership of this type means that you alone own and control the use and distribution of this asset during your life. Upon death, the assets of which you are the sole owner are transferred to your heirs by the terms of your last will and testament. This is the way a lot of my widows and single people own their assets. You can change the terms of a last will and testament at any time as a way of changing the distribution of these assets.

Let's say you go to the bank and move the money from a CD into an *annuity.* An annuity contract requires the designation of a beneficiary and will no longer pass via the terms of your will. If you name a different beneficiary, you have just changed your estate plan and may not even realize it! Only if you make your estate the beneficiary will it follow the terms of your will.

Joint ownership: This type of ownership may be in several forms. It is important to determine which type you have selected:

• *Joint tenancy by the entirety:* is reserved for assets owned by a married couple. Owners share an undivided interest in the property during their lifetimes. Gifting or selling this property requires the consent of both parties. At the death of one owner, the property automatically transfers to the surviving owner by operation of law and does not follow the terms of the decedent's last will and testament.

• *Joint tenancy with rights of survivorship (JTWROS):* is the most common form of joint ownership and is probably the way the bank opened your account if it is jointly held with your son or daughter. Owners share an equal one-half share (moiety) during life, and the surviving owner receives the property by operation of law at the death of the other joint owner.

Many people think it is a good idea to put their child on their account with them to make it easier for them to write checks and to avoid probate. Depending on the parties involved and the amount of money in the account, this may work just fine. However, there are things to consider before you do this.

Does your child have creditors or could he be sued? If so, this money could be accessed by them. Do you expect your child to share this money with your other children after you die? Your child does not legally have to do this unless the other children can prove the joint account was established only as "a convenience." Naturally, this would require hiring a lawyer and going to court.

• ***Joint tenancy in common*** *(JTIC):* allows more than one person to own part of an asset at the same time. This is the default type of joint account if the title does not indicate rights of survivorship. With this type of joint account, any owner can transfer his or her interest without the consent of the other owners. At death, each owner's interest passes through his estate (most likely through the terms of his will).

I have a 92-year-old client who inherited a piece of property with his sister. Unfortunately, the deed did not indicate that they were to inherit it as joint tenants with rights of survivorship. Consequently, they own it as tenants in common, meaning each owns an undivided one-half. Now that his sister has passed away, we have to open a probate estate for her before we can transfer the property out of her name. If his sister's will named someone other than her brother, or if she died without a will and he was not her heir, there would be further complications and costs to transfer her half of the property into his name.

Contractual ownership *(designated beneficiaries):* Many people do not realize that when they buy an annuity, they are signing a contract with an insurance company. Similarly, your retirement account is invested under the terms of a contract. In both cases, you are asked to designate a beneficiary to receive the proceeds when you die. This contract controls the distribution of the asset, regardless of any provisions made in your will. Therefore, it is important to coordinate these distributions with the rest of your estate plan. Other contractual or beneficiary-designated assets include life insurance and individual retirement accounts (IRAs).

Living trust *(also called revocable trust):* This is a document created by an individual while he is alive. Trusts allow for the separation of the legal and beneficial ownership of an asset. The trustee owns the assets and invests and maintains them for the benefit of the beneficiary of the trust. For purposes of asset management, living trusts can be a very effective way of titling assets. This concept will be thoroughly reviewed in the next chapter.

What Else Should You Know?

If you go to an estate planning attorney who does not review the title and ownership of all of your assets, do not go back. Find an attorney who will walk you through this process. It will help everyone to better understand the current status of your plan and see whether your assets would transfer the way you intended. This is a good place to begin the distribution discussion. If you or your parents are like many of my clients, gathering and disclosing this information to one person may never have been done before.

It's funny how secretive people are about showing anyone "all their stuff." Most people have assets in many places, and different financial professionals may each know only part of the picture. It is, however, critical that someone understands the whole picture. Whether it is the Medicaid office or the executor, it will all be added up at some point—often with surprising results.

A good estate planning attorney will review the current asset situation and explain what would happen to each asset when one or both parents become ill or die. An even better attorney would call in your investment adviser or one they could recommend, and complete the process with everyone together.

How Much Do You Have Squirreled Away?

Now that you have gathered in one place all of the information regarding what you own and how it is titled, you may be surprised to see how much is actually there. This may also be the first time that you give yourself permission to think about what you would like to do with it all. Most estate plans focus on death and the transfer of assets at that time, which we will discuss throughout this book. Hopefully, you still have time to make some good decisions about how to use and enjoy your accumulated wealth before your children inherit it!

Some people can't even think about enjoying their money themselves. They only want to leave it for their children. That's OK—at least we have an objective upon which to focus. Let's say the choices were to enjoy some of it yourself now, or to spend it all on a nursing home at the end of your life. Doesn't a new car sound like more fun?

Be honest about your lifestyle and budget. Are you still accumulating money each month from excess income you don't spend? Are you limiting yourself just so as not to touch your "savings"? When is your rainy day finally going to come? Perhaps you can think of some fun and memorable ways to enjoy the money with your family now, instead of keeping it all hidden away until your death. The memories of a big family vacation will last long after you are gone and longer than it would take for them to spend their inheritance on something of which you may never have approved!

An estate planning attorney may or may not ask you to consider what you plan to do between now and your death. This is because the focus is usually on taxes, probate, and who gets what. But this is the time to consider how you would like your story to end. Leaving your children the most money may not be the only consideration as you plan for the coming years and the trials that come with getting older. Consider what your money means to you and how it will best serve you and your family from now until you die.

Do You Have Any Estate Taxes to Consider?

Another reason to spend a little more now may be because you would owe estate taxes if you died with everything you currently own. In the United States, the estate tax has been part of death since 1916. Basically, the government adds up everything you own at death and subjects it to one final tax. The amounts of monies that individuals can leave to the next generation without paying an estate tax have dramatically increased in recent years.

At the federal level, each individual can now transfer approximately $5 million at death before having to pay any estate tax. The federal estate tax rates are high—close to 50 percent—but do not affect most people. It is also important to note that not all assets in an estate are taxed. For example, you can leave any amount of property to your spouse free from federal and state estate taxes. Also, gifts to charities are not taxable.

Some states impose their own estate or inheritance taxes. For example, until this year, New York State imposed an estate tax on assets of more than $1 million. That number brought estate taxes into view for many people who had large retirement plans or real estate holdings. Life insurance is also counted as part of your taxable estate, which comes as a surprise to many clients. If you own the policy, even though it transfers tax-free to your heirs, the amount is included in your taxable estate for calculation purposes.

One way people can reduce estate taxes is to make gifts of assets during their lifetimes. Of course, there are rules—you can't just decide to give it all away on your deathbed. You can give an unlimited amount during your life, but if you give more than $14,000 (currently) to any one individual in one year, you must file a gift tax return with the IRS. The amount over $14,000 will be deducted from your $5 million lifetime gift-and-estate-tax exclusion. A husband and wife can each give up to $14,000 annually to the same individual under current law.

This allows for creative planning for very wealthy individuals and their advisers. Most people with less than $5 million don't need to worry about gift taxes because they can't give away enough money to ever owe a tax. It is important to note that you cannot make any of these gifts under the Medicaid rules without creating problems. We will discuss this in later chapters. I will be repeating this, but it continues to confuse many of my clients: You cannot make $14,000 annual gifts without incurring penalties if you plan to apply for Medicaid.

Who Gets What, and When?

It's true, estate planning has to do with minimizing estate taxes and administration costs. However, there are many other aspects of planning:

- whom would you like to receive the benefits of your estate?

- financially speaking, how will your spouse be without you?

- what are the circumstances and needs of your children and grandchildren?

Think about your children's experience managing their own money and about their competence (or lack thereof) to manage the investments you might leave to them. Remember, you won't be here to help them anymore.

People have widely differing views about how and when to give money to their children. Most people I've met have been generous throughout their lives, helping some of their children when they needed it. Whether the other siblings know how much each has received can make the final distribution easier or harder. Some people don't care about making it "fair" and may even express the desire to give additional help to those who are not as successful as their other children. In contrast, the brothers and sisters usually do care.

Old sibling rivalries seem to resurface around this issue and emotions can run high. Some of the worst displays of human behavior can be found when families start fighting over an estate. Your family has a dynamic that has been created over the years as events have occurred. How you structure your estate at death can either reinforce healthy aspects of your family, or fuel the flames of conflict that may already exist.

Remember that your estate plan may include assets that transfer directly to heirs outside the terms of your will. You may have added a child to your checking or savings account. This account will transfer directly to him or her upon your death. Your child is under no legal obligation to share it with his or her siblings. There is no explanation that gets sent with the check to the beneficiary of your account labeled "transfer on death to …." Consequently, if the amounts are not equal from different accounts that you have established for each child, you may have avoided probate but contributed to family conflicts after your death.

Your estate plan communicates things to your heirs, like who is important, whom you trust, and who deserves to get what. The distribution of your estate carries added emotional weight because it is your final statement. Unlike previous poor decisions you may have made, this time you cannot rectify the mistakes or oversights. Working out a thoughtful plan shows that you care about your family and its cohesiveness after you are gone. Considering the emotions involved in these decisions, it is important to have an objective adviser with whom you can communicate freely and discuss your options.

In my opinion, after working with clients and having been through this myself, your most valuable asset is your family. Sometimes there is nothing that you can do to repair distorted perceptions of past unfairness or favoritism. Furthermore, the current state of your family relations will most likely influence how you feel about what to do next. Just remember to think about how these decisions will affect the family that remains after you are gone.

Every family is unique. Your estate planning attorney needs to know all about it. If you are in a second marriage, you need to know about laws that may require you to leave at least a portion of your estate to your current spouse. If you leave it all to her, she may have no desire to leave any to your natural children from your first marriage. That may be fine with you, but at least you should know what could happen if this is your plan.

Even if your children understand the concern you have for the welfare of your surviving spouse, they may feel left out if their inheritance is not considered. What about the personal things they want to have from you that may be in the house your new wife now occupies?

Do you have a disabled child? Many people decide not to leave anything to this child so as not to have her lose her government benefits. This may not be the best solution. Leaving money to another child to hold for his disabled sibling may not work out either. What if the well child is sued or suffers bankruptcy? There is a special trust you can establish in your will to benefit a disabled person that will not affect his or her government benefits. You need to discuss these situations with a good estate planning attorney.

Have you made loans to some of your children that you expect them to pay back? Would you prefer to have those loans forgiven? Your other children may know about these issues but not know how you want them handled.

What happens if one or more of your children pass away before you? Because people are living longer, children are often well into their adulthood when their parents pass away. Sometimes, unfortunately, children die before their parents. Beneficiary designations should always have a successor listed. Your will should clearly provide what should happen if your child is not alive. If your grandchildren are young, trusts can be created to hold, manage, and use the assets for their benefit until they are older. You may want to stipulate that another one of your children will serve as trustee over this family money. Do you have children or grandchildren who tend to make unwise money decisions? This may be another reason to establish a trust that is created under the terms of your will.

Some of your assets are unique, too. What about the vacation home? I have clients with some children who really love to visit the lake and others who live far away. It would be a shame to have the

MONEY DOESNT BRING YOU HAPPINESS

family cottage sold to equalize the distribution just because you did not leave explicit instructions for your family to follow.

So, you can see that there is a lot to consider about how your assets will transfer upon your death. But planning for your death is just the beginning! Isn't this fun? The more money you have, the more plans we have to make. Maybe you should go shopping or take a trip so we will have less work to do!

The next chapter will help you understand some of the documents and techniques used to transfer assets during your lifetime or at your death.

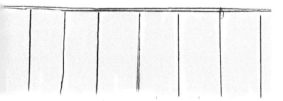

3

BASIC DOCUMENTS
OF AN ESTATE PLAN

HIS CHAPTER DESCRIBES the following common documents associated with establishing an estate plan:

- power of attorney
- health-care proxy
- living will
- last will and testament
- trusts (revocable and irrevocable)
- deed transfer with a retained life estate.

Your plan may include some or all of these documents. They should be drawn up by someone who takes the time to explain your options and the reasons you should have them.

For example, some people have a revocable, or living, trust but think it is the same thing as an irrevocable trust. Make sure you understand the differences and why you are using one form of trust instead of another. If I only had a dime for every client with an old will that uses the term "per stirpes" but still doesn't know what it means.

Power of attorney: This is one of several documents called *advance directives,* which designate and provide instructions to the people who will manage your affairs if you become unable to do so yourself. This document should always be completed as part of a basic estate plan.

Older people often come to my office having updated their will but having failed to execute a power of attorney at the same time. I can't overemphasize how important the power-of-attorney document can be and how crucial it is that it be completed correctly. By its terms, you (the principal) nominate someone to be your *agent* or *attorney-in-fact* who can legally act on your behalf. Your agent must be specifically granted the powers to complete future transactions by the terms of this document.

Each state has a different law regarding the assignment of financial powers, but there are important general guidelines. You should consult with an attorney who specializes in elder law in your state to complete this form. It is essential that the document you sign is legally sufficient to grant the necessary authorizations for your agent to act on your behalf. Some states require the agent named in the document to sign and accept the responsibility before the document becomes effective. The authorization signed by the agent might need to be notarized, putting her on notice of her duties and obligations with respect to her role as agent.

Among other requirements, the agent must follow the instructions of the principal, when known, or to otherwise act in his or her best interest. This first requirement helps the agent understand that she is acting as a *fiduciary*—someone entrusted to hold and manage the money of another—for the principal. Fiduciaries are held to a high standard of responsibility.

By accepting this role, the fiduciary is agreeing to act on behalf of a friend or relative and manage his or her money the way that person would have. She must follow any plans that person already had in place, like the ultimate distribution of assets expressed in the person's last will and testament. This agent cannot change who gets what unless so directed by the principal. For example, she cannot put all of the money in a joint account with herself and keep it if the principal had intended to benefit a charity after his or her death.

The power-of-attorney form can authorize the agent to transfer assets or make gifts. In some states, like New York, the gifting power may be separated from the rest of the document. I have seen many documents signed without authorizing this power, which can cause problems should assets need to be di-

I can't overemphasize how important the power-of-attorney document can be and how crucial it is that it be completed correctly.

vested in the future. Once someone loses capacity to sign a new power of attorney, the agent can exercise only those powers that he or she has been granted. If you want your agent to be able to transfer assets or make gifts on your behalf to preserve these assets, that specific authority must be granted. Unless modified, the form usually creates a *durable power of attorney.* This means it becomes effective when it is executed by all of the parties and remains effective even if the principal should become incapacitated. That is the real benefit of the document. It does not take away your ability to act on your own behalf while you are able. However, it is there should something happen that leaves you needing help managing your financial affairs.

Statutory power-of-attorney forms can be modified to include powers like the ability to apply for government benefits or to establish or revoke a trust. You should specifically authorize actions that your agent may have to undertake, like updating beneficiary designations and doing Medicaid planning.

Attorneys who practice in elder law have already encountered the issues that may come up and have included language in their documents that provide for these events. The form that you might get from the Internet or your attorney-friend who is doing you a favor will likely not have these provisions.

So, you have an old power-of-attorney document that you believe is still good. Does your agent know that she has been named to act on your behalf? Does she understand the responsibility that being your agent entails? Does your agent know what you own and where the assets are located? As we go through life, we tend to accumulate various accounts at different banks and other financial institutions. Do you have an organized list of your current investments? It is important that the agent is made aware of them in order to be able to do the job. The agent should know your plan and the names and numbers of your financial consultants and your estate planning attorney. The requirement that your agent sign the form at least puts her on notice to ask these questions. A good idea would be to involve the agent in your estate planning discussions.

Many people want to know if they can name more than one agent to act on their behalf. This is possible and you should carefully consider whom and why you appoint these individuals. The job of being someone's financial agent should not be given to a child just because that child is the oldest or because she will get upset if she is not named. Who is always there to help you and is involved with your current affairs? Is he financially capable and responsible with his own money? If you plan on naming more than one agent, can they work together effectively? You might consider naming one agent and then another as a successor, should the first agent become unable to do the work.

This can become a sticky situation for some families. Everyone has different talents and personalities. Sometimes one child has the financial acumen to do the job, but may not have the time to take on the responsibility of managing your finances, given her own busy life. If you most trust the child who is out of town, that person can still do the job, given the online capabilities now available to us all. This is an important decision. It should be made by considering what is in your best interest and not made out of a feeling of obligation.

A health-care proxy allows you to legally appoint someone to act as your health-care agent when you can't make decisions yourself about your care.

Remember, your power of attorney (agent) acts on your behalf during your lifetime. He or she may or may not be your executor who acts under the authority given in your last will and testament. These are different responsibilities and they can be given to different people, but they are often the same person.

It will be much better for you to decide who will handle this important task, rather than leaving it up to others should something happen to you. If you haven't designated someone in writing, a guardianship proceeding may have to be conducted to make this decision. This will be expensive and may not result in the decision you would have made, given the choice.

Health-care proxy: This advance directive is for health-care decision making. Your power-of-attorney document does not give your agent any authority over your health care. Most states have codified the ability for you to delegate health-care authority by legislation that created a statutory form for a health-care proxy.

Your health-care proxy is the document that allows you to legally appoint someone to act as your health-care agent if you are unable to speak for yourself to make health-care decisions. Your agent will be allowed to make decisions on your behalf only after your doctor determines that you are no longer able to make health-care decisions yourself. Your agent will have authority to make all decisions about your health care, unless you limit his authority. He will be able to make decisions about whether to use or remove treatments that may extend your life and which tests and surgeries will be allowed.

A place on the form allows you to specify these instructions. It is important that you write down your instructions regarding artificial nutrition and hydration (i.e., providing feeding or hydration through a tube) so that your agent is able to follow your instructions regarding these difficult decisions.

The most important qualification for your agent is that he will follow your wishes, even if he does not agree. These are your decisions that the agent will be enacting for you. Obviously, this person needs to be someone you trust.

Next, consider whether this person will be available when you need help making these decisions. Is this person capable of interacting with medical personnel and understanding the conditions and choices being discussed? Will she be able to demand that your wishes be followed? You want to have a good advocate for your care decisions when you are not able to speak for yourself. Furthermore, this is not a one-time discussion. As your age and health conditions change, your thoughts about treatments may also change. Make sure to keep your agent updated as your decisions evolve over time.

Comment: Use your state's statutory form for a health-care proxy because it will be most easily recognized. If you have one drawn up for you by your attorney, make sure that you read it and that you agree with any "standard language" that they may have put in their form.

Living will: Because of its name, a living will is often confused with living trusts and other documents. The basic purpose of a living will is to allow you to provide instructions to your health-care representative (proxy) and medical personnel regarding life-sustaining treatment. This document can instruct them to withdraw these treatments if you become terminally ill or are in a persistent vegetative state.

This document becomes effective only when you are incapacitated. It can be revoked. By using a living will, you make your care preferences known. It will still be up to your health-care agent to make sure that your wishes are carried out when you are unable to speak for yourself. This document, however, is not enforceable in some states. In this case, it simply helps your health-care agent make difficult decisions, knowing that they were your intentions while you had the ability to speak for yourself.

Last will and testament: Everyone knows they should have a will and many people do. That doesn't prevent most people from holding common misconceptions about this basic estate planning document.

To be considered valid, a will must follow certain formalities:

- it must be in writing
- it must be signed at the end in the presence of two witnesses, who must also sign the will
- the creator of the will must also declare it to be his or her will in the witnesses' presence.

The person signing the will must know the approximate nature and value of his or her assets and who are the objects of his bounty (i.e., the people he or she wants to benefit). If your last will and testament is to be allowed by the court, it must meet certain standards. Remember, you will not be here to clarify your intentions. People might argue about any ambiguities. If you want to make changes, go back and discuss these with your adviser. There may be a better way to accomplish your new goals that you hadn't previously considered.

But I Don't Want Probate!

The most common misconception is that your will directs the disposition of all of your property. The truth is, your will directs only the disposition of your probate property. "Oh, no!" I hear you cry, "but I don't want probate." Unfortunately, probate is the process that your will must undergo to be proven valid by the surrogate, or probate, court.

Think about it for a minute. If there was no entity that had the ultimate authority to determine which will or statement was your last expression of your wishes, people holding "older" wills could get to the bank first and get the money before the "newer" document might be presented. So, the will is not the actual document that gets presented to the institutions holding your assets.

Let's say you signed a will 10 years ago leaving everything to your brother. Then last year you changed your mind and made a new will that gives everything to your sister. Then you died. Your brother knew about the first will, obtained a copy from the attorney who drafted it, and took it to the bank. The next day, your sister took the newest will to the bank and told them she is to receive the money now that you have passed. But the banker has

It is extremely important for all of your estate advisers to communicate and work together to accomplish your goals.

told her that your brother came in the day before with a different will that left it all to him, so now the money is gone.

The possible existence of multiple wills and other problems, like undue influence or fraud, require that your will must first be proven in court to have been properly drafted and executed. The people who would have received your property had you died without a will are given an opportunity to object to the will at that time. After a court proceeding to determine that the will is the valid last expression of your wishes, your executor is then given *letters testamentary,* which allow him to transfer your assets according to the directions you have given in your will.

Many of my clients are also concerned about hurting children's feelings when they select one child to be executor of their will. In reality, the executor is required to follow the terms of your will and does not have discretion to make decisions that would favor himself or herself, unless you leave those decisions up to him or her.

Again, it will probably be a better decision to select a child who knows how to handle paperwork and finances rather than a child who has trouble managing his own affairs. Similarly, you may want to choose the child who has the time to take on this extra task, instead of the child who has three young children of his own and lives in another state. Decisions have to be made and they should be made thoughtfully. You won't be here to make sure it all works out the way you would like. Choose the person you think is most likely to ensure that your wishes are fulfilled.

What if you don't want to leave equal amounts to your children? Can you "disinherit" someone? In most states, only your spouse has a "right" to inherit from you. If you do not leave him or her anything, he or she can claim *right of election* against your estate. This means that the spouse would inherit one-third of your total assets at the time of your death.

Furthermore, your children do not have a "right" to inherit anything from you. As an example, you can simply state in your will that you have purposely not provided for that person "for personal reasons." This prevents her from claiming that you "forgot" her. If your will is properly drafted by a competent attorney, this should work fine.

A better way to accomplish this may be to use *will substitutes* to distribute your property. These allow your estate to avoid court involvement and the requirement that disinherited children be given a chance to object to your will. If you were to name beneficiaries for your assets that were paid directly to them by the terms of a contract, your will would not come into play. For example, proceeds from annuities or life insurance are paid to the beneficiaries listed on the contract, regardless of the terms of your will.

I should probably mention here the consequences of marriages later in life. As mentioned previously, people are living longer. Many of my clients find another person to love after the death of their first spouse.

How a Will and Revocable Trust Work

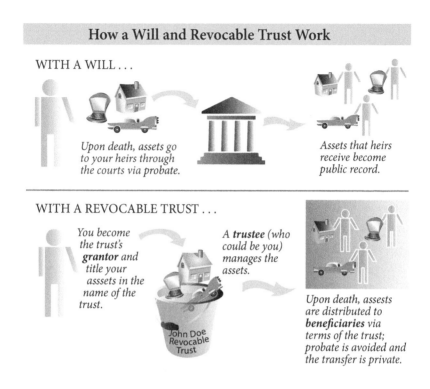

WITH A WILL...

Upon death, assets go to your heirs through the courts via probate.

Assets that heirs receive become public record.

WITH A REVOCABLE TRUST...

You become the trust's **grantor** and title your asssets in the name of the trust.

A **trustee** (who could be you) manages the assets.

Upon death, assests are distributed to **beneficiaries** via terms of the trust; probate is avoided and the transfer is private.

John Doe Revocable Trust

Love is a blessing whenever it is found. However, if not fully understood, marrying later in life can result in unintended financial complications for both parties. As you will see in the chapter on paying for long-term care, spouses are responsible for each other's long-term care costs. In addition, upon death, the surviving spouse is entitled to the right of election we have discussed. If you plan on remarrying later in life, be sure that you understand the financial ramifications of doing so.

Trusts: People often think trusts are complicated and difficult to understand. In reality, they are just the opposite.

Think of a trust like a bucket. It has writing on the outside that contains all the instructions for what to do and what not to do with the assets put inside of it. Your trustee will follow those instructions and take care of the assets that you place in the bucket. Some of the reasons you may use a trust to hold your assets include:

- removing assets from your ownership to another entity
- allowing someone else to manage your assets for you, if you are unable
- making the transactions private and avoiding probate.

A trust is the document that gives the instructions about what to do with the assets that are governed by its terms. The *grantor* (or *donor*) is the person who puts the assets into the trust. The *trustee* is the person named in the document to carry out the instructions of the grantor. The *beneficiaries* are the people who will benefit from the trust. It's that simple.

A trust can be either *revocable*—you can make changes to it at any time, or take all of the assets out, or put assets in whenever you like—or *irrevocable*, which means there are certain restrictions on the actions you can take regarding the assets.

• ***Revocable trust:*** These trusts allow you to retain complete control over the assets held by the trust during your lifetime. You are allowed to amend, revoke, or terminate the trust at any time. You can change the terms of the trust or take all of the money out.

In every trust document there are three principal parties. First, we have the grantors. They create the trust and transfer their assets into it. Next, we have the trustees. They are in charge of managing the assets in the trust. Trustees make all the financial and management decisions regarding the trust assets (according to the instructions written by the grantors in the trust document). For example, the trustee usually has the right to buy, sell, transfer, exchange, and otherwise manage the assets. The beneficiaries receive the benefits of the assets according to the terms of the trust. If the trustee is also a beneficiary, he can spend the money on himself and use the trust assets for his own benefit. That is usually the job reserved for the third party, the beneficiaries. The trust itself is simply the written agreement between you (the grantor) and the trustee about what can be done with the assets placed under its control. The trust document typically includes instructions about how to manage the assets during your lifetime and how they should be distributed at death.

You may have a vacation home in another state. This is a great reason to use a revocable trust.

In the case of a revocable trust, the grantor, trustee, and beneficiary can all be the same person. The trust document names a successor trustee to act if or when something happens to you, such as incapacity or death. The next trustee then steps in and continues to manage the property in the trust according to your written instructions.

Let's say you understand the concept of a revocable trust and have determined that it might be something that fits your planning needs. The trust document itself is so important that it must be drafted by someone who will create it to fit your specific needs. There are some legal provisions that will need to be included in the document to make it work, but its expression can be so flexible that you really need an attorney with whom you can readily communicate to draft it for you. There are many attorneys who have cookie-cutter trusts that will do it for you cheaply. However, the language may not be right for you or your intentions. Some people use online document-drafting systems and try to do it themselves. I would not recommend either of these approaches.

If you are thinking about using a trust, find an adviser who will work with you until you understand how the trust will function and who will see that it does what you want it to do. For example, you may have a vacation home in another state. This is a great reason to use a revocable trust. By changing the ownership from you to the trust, you can avoid *ancillary probate*, which would otherwise occur after your death if property is owned in other states.

Furthermore, the validity of your last will and testament will have to be proven through the probate process in the state where the property is located. That can become very expensive and time-consuming. If you want the property to remain in the family, you can explain how it should be used and managed by your heirs in the future through the terms of the trust document. As a result, nothing should have to be brought to court in that state.

Another reason that you should use a qualified attorney to create your trust is that the document itself is only one of the

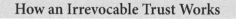

How an Irrevocable Trust Works

By removing assets from your ownership, an irrevocable trust puts you in a better position to qualify for Medicaid sooner than you would if your assets were not in the trust, while preserving those assets for your heirs.

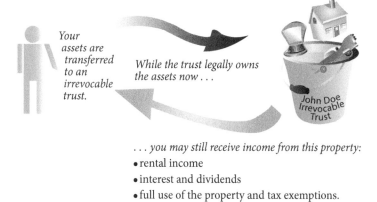

Your assets are transferred to an irrevocable trust.

While the trust legally owns the assets now . . .

John Doe Irrevocable Trust

. . . you may still receive income from this property:
- rental income
- interest and dividends
- full use of the property and tax exemptions.

parts that makes the trust work. You still have to put the assets in the "bucket" (i.e., "fund" the trust). The trust can control only assets that are retitled—in other words, owned by the trust.

I have lost count of the number of my clients who have taken the time and paid good money to create a revocable trust but have never transferred ownership of their assets to the trust. Consequently, the trust is of no use. Once you have a trust, it is important that all your advisers know about it and your reasons for establishing it. Some people create a trust to avoid probate and then proceed to purchase additional assets (such as annuities) that have beneficiary designations that do not coordinate with the distribution of their trust.

• ***Irrevocable trust:*** These trusts are used to remove assets from your ownership, for various planning reasons. They should not be confused with revocable trusts—they are used for very different purposes. The idea of putting assets into a trust is to change the legal ownership of the asset from you to the trust. As is the case with revocable trusts, the assets held in an irrevocable trust will avoid probate when you die. However, an irrevocable trust removes the asset from your control during your lifetime. Why would you want to do that?

One of the most common reasons we use an irrevocable trust is for long-term care planning. Under current Medicaid law, five years after assets have changed ownership to an irrevocable trust, they will not be considered available to pay for your care.

As I will explain in a later chapter, Medicaid is a needs-based program that can pay for long-term care. To qualify for these benefits, an applicant must meet certain asset and income requirements. If you don't have long-term care insurance, you have to *spend down* your assets until you meet the program requirements. An irrevocable trust can hold assets outside of your name, allow you to qualify for Medicaid, and still have those assets transfer to your heirs after you die.

By using an irrevocable trust, you can preserve the principal of the transferred assets and still have access to the income generated by those assets to help you with your regular living expenses. When properly drafted, the trust will allow the trustee to access the principal of the trust during your lifetime for the benefit of your children or other beneficiaries, but the trustee cannot give principal directly back to you. You can also keep the

Deed Transfer With Retained Life Estate: *How It Works*

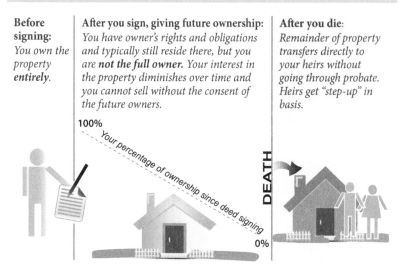

Before signing: *You own the property **entirely**.*

After you sign, giving future ownership: *You have owner's rights and obligations and typically still reside there, but you are **not the full owner**. Your interest in the property diminishes over time and you cannot sell without the consent of the future owners.*

After you die: *Remainder of property transfers directly to your heirs without going through probate. Heirs get "step-up" in basis.*

100%

Your percentage of ownership since deed signing

DEATH

0%

authority to change the ultimate beneficiaries of the trust (called a *power of appointment*) by reappointing them to different people, as beneficiaries, in the future.

You can transfer your residence into this trust and retain the exclusive right to use and occupy the premises. If the trust is properly drafted, you can maintain all of your senior citizen and veterans real estate tax exemptions. The trustee can even sell your home and purchase another for you with the proceeds. Similarly, the proceeds can be invested to generate more income for your use.

The irrevocable trust has many benefits over an outright transfer of assets to your heirs. If you give your assets away, your beneficiaries can spend them or lose them to creditors. Also, they receive the assets with your cost basis at the time of transfer. That means they will be responsible for any taxes due on the increase in value from the time that you purchased them. These capital gains can be avoided by waiting to actually transfer the assets to your beneficiaries at the time of your death, as with the trust.

The most common reasons for using an irrevocable trust are to:

- avoid probate for the assets held in the trust
- manage the assets held in the trust if the grantor becomes unable to do so
- protect the assets from creditors and nursing-home costs
- hold assets to be given at a later time, but remove them from ownership now
- maintain privacy as to what happens to the assets.

Deed transfer with retained life estate: Many people want to know how to protect the equity in their house from the costs of long-term care to make sure that their children at least receive their house as an inheritance. Property laws can be confusing because of tax and capital gains issues, as well as transfer penalties relating to long-term care planning. Be sure you understand the consequences of any transfer you make and that the documents are completed by someone who understands this type of law.

Real property is treated differently under the law from other assets. Because land is permanent, it is unlike many other assets you may own and is transferred differently. For example, you can give someone ownership of your property for a period of time, even in the future. That is the crux of a property transfer with retained

I hear people say that they already "gave my house to my kids." I always hope that is not literally what they have done.

life-estate technique. You can divide the ownership of land over time. This means you can keep the ownership of your property during your lifetime and deed the future ownership to someone else.

I hear people say that they already "gave my house to my kids." I always hope that is not literally what they have done. Most likely, they have signed a deed that gives their children the remainder interest in their property while retaining a life estate for themselves. This technique allows people to give their children the ownership now of a property interest that will be in place after their death.

By doing this, the parents can maintain all the current rights and obligations of ownership, like paying the taxes, collecting the rents, and benefiting from government tax exemptions. But if someone asks if they own their home, they can legally say that they no longer own the entire interest in the property. The property is now legally owned by their children after the parents' life estate ends, at their death, without the need to do anything else. After this type of transfer, you will need the consent of all the future owners to sell the property.

If you are at all concerned about the financial stability of your children or their propensity to sign a sales agreement during your lifetime, I would not advise this type of outright transfer. You may want to use a trust that reserves a life estate for you and transfers the remainder to your children after you are gone. This will avoid the probate process for the property and it will be protected from being used to pay for your long-term care costs after five years.

For example, your one son is financially unstable and could potentially face bankruptcy in the future. His future interest in the property ownership will be recorded when the deed is filed. That ownership interest is subject to his creditors, who can place a lien upon the property for when it is sold in the future. In this case, you should make sure that the deed contains a "power of appointment" clause. This clause would allow you to rename the beneficiaries of the property and remove the child who is in financial trouble before he files for bankruptcy.

If the parents think they may want to sell the property before their death, it is important to understand that the owners of the future interest in the property must also agree to the sale. The proceeds from the sale would be proportionally divided, using the sale price and current life-expectancy tables to determine the shares. The sellers who do not live on the property at the time of sale would be subject to capital gains taxes on their profit.

For all these reasons, it is important to discuss this planning technique with a competent adviser who practices in this area of law. It may turn out that the property should be placed into an irrevocable trust to accomplish the desired result. But each situation and family are different. I use both techniques regularly, depending on the facts.

How This All Fits Together

So now we have reviewed some of the basic things you want to know to get started on an estate plan. Some of the documents and legal techniques we have discussed will play a part in the control and management of your assets while you are still alive. However, there is a lot more that we should plan for if we are going to successfully make it through our elderhood.

Asset management and distribution are going to play a part in the process, but family interactions and the potential need for long-term care support in some form will have a lot to do with the success of any plan. Now is the time to meet and discuss your thoughts about this next stage of your life with people who can help you put it all together. Let me give you an example:

Let's say Mom and Dad had their family attorney draft their wills and establish power-of-attorney documents for each other. Their assets are mostly at the bank, and they have purchased several annuities through their financial institution. Now that Dad has been showing some sign of dementia, the local kids want to help get things in order. Who can help?

Their family attorney may not be aware that the power of attorney he drafted needs to have the gifts rider, a separate clause authorizing Mom to move assets from Dad's name, should we need to get him on a Medicaid program in the future. The banker may not know that the annuities will have special rules applied to them for Medicaid purposes. Furthermore, who knows how many banks are holding Mom and Dad's accounts? In addition to sorting out the money, we have to get Mom some relief from watching Dad 24 hours a day. The local kids are trying to help, but they have family and work obligations that leave Mom to manage on her own most of the time. The television and Internet provide some information about care that might be available. You can also ask friends or call senior services. However, all the pieces are getting harder to put together.

Wouldn't it be great if there were one place where you could discuss and organize all of this for the best possible outcome for everyone? Our current system does not do this well. It takes a dedicated professional (who may have been through the process with her own family) and many others to know what is needed and how to get there. Ideally, this is someone who will help families sort through their care needs while working with the legal and financial situations that need to be addressed.

Unfortunately, not everyone gets to have such a person as his or her resource and guide. The next chapters will provide information about the types of care that should be available and how to pay for them. However, I will continue to emphasize the need to find someone in your area who can help you through the process. If we are lucky enough to have our parents live into old age, we will all probably go through some of these situations. We can help each other by sharing what we know and getting the right advice as soon as possible.

4

ALL IN THE FAMILY

LL OF THIS IS PERSONAL. Every issue that we will discuss in the course of planning for families has the potential for obvious or unexpected conflict. We are talking about families, and not one of them is "normal."

Families are made up of people who are related, but may be as different from each other as strangers. Members of every family were born in different generations and undoubtedly have had very different life experiences. Each individual will see the same discussion from a unique perspective.

As altruistic as we all hope to be, everyone looks at the problem from his or her own point of view. Depending on the strength of personality or level of interest a person has on any given issue, things may go smoothly or conflicts may arise.

Take the local child who has taken on most of the responsibility for caring for her parents. This may be because she wants

Even in a loving family, simple distance and lack of regular communication can make decisions about long-term care more difficult.

this responsibility or because she is the only one left in town. While at first she may be only helping Mom with cooking or shopping, her role may soon evolve into paying the bills. This "caregiver" child may begin feeling stressed about the extra time it takes every week to handle these tasks. The last thing she is thinking about is how her out-of-town brother feels about all of this. This brother is an accountant and has been named Mom's power of attorney. He isn't being consulted now about Mom's finances and is concerned that she is spending too much on groceries lately.

What if this sister had recently consulted an elder law attorney about preparing for a potential Medicaid application and learned that money should no longer be given to the children? When her brother flies home to see how things are going, she tells him Mom won't be able to reimburse his airline ticket like she always has. Here we go. The sister thinks she is doing the right thing for Mom. The brother feels like she has taken over an area of control he expected to have.

Even if Mom is still capable of making decisions about such tasks, she may not want to get involved in the conflict. Even though she had executed a power of attorney giving her son authority over her finances, she has made her daughter a joint owner on her checking and savings account. Communication and education will be the key to success in this situation. Many families are not well informed, much less good at discussing things with each other. Even in a loving family, simple distance and lack of regular communication can make these issues more difficult.

In my family, it seemed obvious that I would be the one to help Mom and Dad. I moved back to Buffalo to attend law school and lived with my parents during that time. After I married and started an elder law and estate planning practice, my husband and I built our house on land directly behind my parents. In some ways (the most important ones) it was the best decision I could have made. I was able to keep my parents together, providing care in their home until they died after 70 years of marriage.

The issues that I can personally say I didn't anticipate (and that surprised me the most) revolved around the care for our parents in the last stages of their lives. For almost 30 years, both my brother and sister have lived in North Carolina. I remember their trying to get my parents to move down there when they were younger, but Bill and Dorothy were not leaving Getzville. Consequently, I was the one who went to the ball games and spent holidays with them. Sibling visits were once or twice a year and no one expected anything different. However, after my dad began having physical issues, decisions needed to be made about his care.

Why did it surprise me that my brother and sister would want to be involved in these discussions? Perhaps it was because I had been the one taking care of them all along, and because I was the one who lived closest, that I thought I would have more say? On the other hand, it may have been because I worked in the field of elder planning, so I thought I should be able to make these decisions without their involvement.

I obviously had a lot to learn about family communication. Ironically, every day clients pay me for advice which invariably includes the need for communication between all interested parties. Why should I think that my brother and sister wouldn't want to be involved? They both loved Mom and Dad as much as I did and wanted to be helpful and feel included. Having bungled through it in my own misguided way, I now see that I was not as objective and altruistic as I had expected I would be. I was dealing with my own feelings of lack of control and helplessness and they were only trying to help. At first it felt like they were just getting in the way. In the end, it worked out better because we were all involved.

The Family and Money

Ready for some fun? This has to be the most booby-trapped area of my work. Everybody has money issues. You may think you don't have money issues, but I'll bet you have money issues. Do you want to talk about your household financial situation with your sister? What makes you think your parents want to talk to you about theirs? Why should they want to talk to their child about their money? (Whether you are 25 or 70, you will still be their child.)

With older generations, discussing finances was generally not done. During the Depression, most parents tried to shield their children from the terrifying fears that shaped their uncertainty about survival. But everyone who went through this stressful period has a different perspective that younger people simply cannot understand. In a few years, most people who went through the Depression will no longer be with us. But many of us are their children.

How can I begin to comprehend why everything seemed too expensive for my parents? They talked about having to sell my mother's wedding dress to buy a potty chair for my sister. I was born 15 years after my brother. But every day that I didn't want to practice for my organ lessons, I was told that I had to because they couldn't afford guitar lessons for Billy. Who thinks like that?

Children of the Depression era have become some of the greatest savers you can imagine. And they hide it. I had one client who was in the hospital and revealed that he had metal boxes of cash buried in his back yard. The financial adviser and I had a hard time getting the Treasury to accept the decayed notes that were all stuck together.

Older people also worried about bank runs. Consequently, I have clients with savings accounts at five or six banks. This may work fine when people are well enough to keep it all organized, but it can become difficult when children have to step in and begin managing their parents' affairs. Sometimes, it takes three or four meetings with me before clients finally reveal the true extent of their financial picture. Ironically, they are asking me for advice! Those of us who have never had a reason to fear that there could be no money may have trouble relating to how they think.

Many of my clients say they don't want to have all their eggs in one basket. As a result, they have accounts at four different local banks and credit unions! I try to get them to see that it is difficult for anyone to advise them on their entire financial picture if given only part of the information. It is like telling your doctor about your high blood pressure but not about your diabetes or cancer diagnosis. As I said, multiple bank accounts can become unwieldy for anyone who has to step in and help with finances in the future. These are things that families should learn about and discuss before financial management becomes an issue.

Some of my clients keep their own spreadsheets and update them personally every month. These people may derive pleasure and security from this time-consuming effort, but most have to turn it over to someone else at some point. Many couples have their own money issues. Sometimes it is a husband who has always controlled the management of the money and the wife has tremendous fear that she cannot understand it without him. She may not want, or be able, to learn it all now, but whom else can she trust?

This is one of the reasons to bring in a professional Dad can relate to, who also can be prepared to help Mom, should Dad become sick or die. Sometimes one parent wants to be more generous with children who have been less successful than their siblings. The other may worry about strife that could result if everyone is not treated equally.

So how do you ever decide who could manage your money as well as you? That is exactly what I am asking when I want clients

It is difficult for anyone to advise people about their financial picture if given only part of the information.

to select someone to be their power of attorney (as reviewed in the last chapter). Without thinking, many couples immediately select the oldest child or their son. Is he the best financial manager of their brood? Does he have the time or interest to become financially responsible for their money when they can no longer handle it?

Given the ease of communication and online financial transactions, proximity is no longer a primary concern. The local child may have never moved out of the house because of her own financial mismanagement or other money issues. Even though these children are "right there," they may not be the best choice. Other parents fear upsetting the oldest child if they select the younger brother who is better at finances. This decision is more important than hurt feelings. I try to get my clients to play out the decision—how will it really work?

Some families may even communicate about financial decisions that need to be made for Mom and Dad after they can no longer manage them by themselves. That's great, but they should still seek the advice from someone familiar with the mistakes they could make. I currently have a family we helped through their dad's illness and nursing-home Medicaid application. The children became painfully aware of the minefield that surrounds the *look-back process* and problems that can arise when gifts are made within five years of a Medicaid application.

However, even after that knowledge, using the authority given to them under a power-of-attorney document, they continued to make gifts from their mom to each of the children over the past several years. They are now running low on funds for private pay for her assisted living and are looking for cheaper places to "put" Mom. This did not have to happen. The situation is very unfortunate.

The Family and Living Arrangements

Just like every other part of this discussion, living arrangements will be as personal as the family involved. Some people grow old without traditional family supports and are lucky to have nieces, nephews, cousins, or even neighbors who are willing to step in. I have older clients in every imaginable living situation. Some older couples remain in their homes for as long as possible until the need for care for one or both becomes too much for them or their families to maintain.

Others, like my parents, can remain at home with caregivers to help the family, but it takes a lot of planning and dedication once the care becomes 24-hour. Some couples decide to move into a *continuing-care retirement community* that has provisions for each level of care as it becomes necessary. This is the easiest plan for people without local family support or for those who choose to plan before the need for care becomes acute. I have some children who build a new house and live together with their parents. Some single folks decide to move to assisted living when they can no longer drive or cook for themselves. The variety and choice of living arrangements have increased dramatically in recent years and will undoubtedly continue to do so as the baby-boom generation continues to age.

Unfortunately, most people don't want to plan for needing care. It is not something we look forward to or expect. All of a sudden, it just happens. I remember it as if it were yesterday. I was outside of the ballpark with Mom, Dad, and my husband. We were waiting for some friends to join us. We always went to the Bisons games. We had a lot of fun together and I would usually drive us all downtown.

We were standing by a lamppost when my father just went down—no warning—not even a sound. He was just on the ground. Thankfully, my husband was there to help get him up. Dad couldn't tell us what he thought had happened or why he fell. We went into the first-aid station, cleaned up the cut to his face, and headed to our seats. We were all confused and stunned about this sudden issue that arose in my otherwise vigorous 91-year-old father. What I didn't recognize at the time was that this was the beginning of the decline process for my dad.

Sometimes it is not a fall or other physical event that forces us to recognize that someone needs help. A child may notice that Mom isn't eating much or has stopped going out with her friends. Maybe she isn't taking her medication regularly. These can be signs of changes taking place and should be questioned. Perhaps she is forgetting things more often. A lot of times, we can simply stop by more frequently and ask some good questions like, "Do you need a little help?" Our parents are just as afraid as we are of these changes. They may not know about all of the help that is available, and that they will not immediately be whisked away to an old folks' home. There are many things that can be done to get our loved ones the help they need before any moves have to take place. The next chapter talks about some of the alternative arrangements that you might not know exist.

5

THERE ARE MANY
LEVELS OF CARE

EW PEOPLE REALLY TALK about the indignities older people suffer. You just get through it. How many times did we slide my father down the hallway on a towel so that he could get his legs below him to get him up after he fell? If I wasn't home, my parents would call the neighbors to help. We weren't yet ready to ask anyone other than family or close friends for advice or assistance. We were "managing" by ourselves. Unfortunately, these falls would soon mean that Dad was becoming unsafe in his own home. How scary is that? Especially when his wife of 68 years just wanted everything to be like it was six months ago.

How do you know when you need outside help? Quite often it takes someone other than a family member to tell you. It might be a doctor at the emergency room or the discharge planner at a rehabilitation center. For us it was the realization that Mom

LEVELS OF CARE

Type of care	What it is, what it typically includes	Level of care, supervision	Includes housing	Cost
SENIOR APARTMENT	A relatively traditional apartment with access to other seniors	None	Yes	Low to mid-range *potential government subsidy*
ADULT DAY CARE	Daytime socialization / entertainment; can include nursing	Low to mid-range	No	Low
RETIREMENT COMMUNITY	Own or rent in a community just for seniors; access to social activities, valet services, emergency call system	Low	Yes	Mid-range to high *depends on level of services*
CONTINUING CARE RETIREMENT COMMUNITY	Buy-in for care for the rest of their lives; includes all levels of care up to skilled nursing	None to very high	Yes	Mid-range to very high *depends on (at first) location / reputation*
IN-HOME CARE	Anything from meal preparation to full-time care, within your home	Low to very high	No	Low to very high *depends on hours of care; **can be paid by Medicaid***
INDEPENDENT LIVING	Access to other seniors, entertainment, emergency call system; meals may be offered	Low to mid-range	Yes	Low to mid-range *depends on level of services*
ASSISTED LIVING	Help with daily activities including medication, meals, hygiene; often includes more socialization, entertainment	Mid-range	Yes	Mid-range *depends on apartment quality and level of care*
RESPITE CARE	Wide range of temporary care in a facility	Low to very high	Yes (short term)	Mid-range to high *depends on daily costs*
DEMENTIA, ALZHEIMER'S CARE	Assisted living (see above) with high level of daily supervision	High	Yes	High to very high
NURSING HOME	Rehabilitation and 24-hour supervision by a skilled staff	High to very high	Yes	High to very high *can be paid by Medicaid*
HOSPICE CARE	Support at end-of-life facility or at home	Very high	May or may not	Paid by Medicare

couldn't do it alone after Dad had to go to the hospital when he fell and hit his head. From there they sent him to rehabilitation. He had just turned 93 and needed to get his strength back.

When my father first came home from rehab, we thought Mom could continue to be the one to make sure he was safe at home. That was how it had always worked; they took care of each other. One day, Dad fell. Then Mom fell while trying to help him. She had broken her pelvis. Now they both needed help. But I needed to be at work to help other people learn how to prepare for the same issues.

I wasn't ready for this. I had their legal documents in place and I knew what they owned and where it was. But the "care" part is often the part that comes as a surprise. You need to know whom to contact when that time comes. This was our time.

So, I called my good friend and colleague who is a geriatric-care manager. I had started our firm as the only law office in Western New York to employ geriatric-care managers. I knew this was going to be an integral part of providing comprehensive services to aging clients and their families. She came over and we arranged to have some aides come to the house to help them.

What Is Long-Term Care?

People use the words "long-term care" as if we all know exactly what we're talking about. It can really mean many different things. Long-term care is a phrase used to describe a wide variety of options provided in many types of settings. It offers services and supports to meet health or personal-care needs over an extended period of time. Long-term care includes all of the supportive *nformal caregivers can get overwhelmed in their attempts to continue as the sole care provider.*

medical, social, and personal services provided to people who cannot perform basic activities of daily living (ADLs). It continues for as long as it is needed. These activities of daily living are usually considered to be:

- bathing
- eating
- dressing
- toileting
- incontinence care
- transferring (such as moving into and out of a chair).

Long-term care basically requires that a healthy person be available to provide support for people who cannot care for themselves as a result of chronic illness or disability. Where the care can be provided, and how much care is necessary, will be determined by the type of disability involved. For example, a man whose wife has had dementia for several years may have cared for her at home by himself. However, he recognizes that he needs outside help once her condition worsens and he can no longer transfer her without assistance.

Or take the wife who has always been able to care for her overweight husband while he could use his walker. Once he cannot stand by himself, she may no longer be able to help him bathe, dress, or use the toilet. She will either need to have help come into the home, or he will have to move into a facility.

Two of the most important things you will need to know about long-term care:

- which services will and will not be provided at each level of care

- in which settings that type of care can be offered.

The costs of care will also be critically important. I will provide a brief overview of payment sources in this chapter and give more detail in the next chapter, "Who Will Pay for All of This?"

Many people associate long-term care with institutionalized care. However, most long-term care is actually provided at home. Even if people eventually need to move to a facility in order to get the care they need, it is usually after care has been administered in the home for a period of time. Most of the care given at this time is provided by *informal caregivers* like family members, friends, and neighbors. Programs like adult day care, transportation, and meal services available in the community often help support the care provided by family and friends.

It is important to understand the progression of care and commitment that may be required. The care plan that satisfies today's needs will probably have to be adjusted repeatedly as the need for care increases. As these changes occur, there is an increased need to add formal caregiving to the informal supports that had worked in the past.

We need to be aware that informal caregivers can get overwhelmed in their attempts to continue as the sole care provider. Sometimes they don't even realize it, sometimes they do but don't want to allow their loved ones to be taken away, and sometimes they fear the costs involved.

Informal care: There is a natural progression that occurs as loved ones become less capable of doing things for themselves. At first, family and friends will stop by more often and help with basic tasks such as preparing meals or cleaning. Every case is different, but this is the beginning of informal care.

• *Intermittent care:* This care is needed to make sure that Mom and Dad are doing OK—that they are getting their meals and taking their medications as prescribed. Everyone is usually still living in his or her own home at this stage. The caregiver usually lives or works close by and can stop in for visits. Even this type of care can be problematic if the natural supports of the elderly person live far away. My brother and sister live in North Carolina. This would have been a problem if I hadn't lived near my parents. In such a case, the children may have to hire a care manager to coordinate the visits by trusted people. I am constantly amazed at how many older people just struggle to get by on their own and are really just one fall away from big changes in their life.

• *Part-time care:* This care may be required numerous times during the day. Mom or Dad might need help getting dressed, bathing, preparing meals, or getting in and out of the bathroom safely. At this stage, it would be difficult for a child to be the only one to help, unless she could live with the parent. If both parents are living, they usually help each other for as long as possible. This can take a significant toll on the physical and emotional health of the spouse providing the care. This strain can even cause the healthy husband or wife to decline (and sometimes die) before their "less-well" spouse.

People in this situation rely on many types of informal care to maintain their life in the community. These services can be done by family members or paid service providers. Types of care provided by informal caregivers include:

- home repairs, lawn mowing, snow removal
- shopping and running errands
- laundry
- transportation to doctors and other appointments
- money management and bill paying
- medication management
- meal preparation
- feeding
- hygiene and grooming
- assistance with walking, dressing, bathing
- wander prevention and home safety
- toileting and managing incontinence.

If a person needs help with only a few of these activities, then the time required by informal caregivers may not be overwhelming. But as the list of needs increases, even people who live with them full time may not be able to keep it up. It is exhausting work to care for someone else all the time. Even for your spouse of 60 years (maybe because that means you are at least 78 when trying to do this), it can get to be too much.

Home-based and community-based services: Many types of programs are available that provide personal support and health services to allow people to remain in their homes for an extended period of time.

• *Adult day-care programs:* These services can offer relief for families by providing the caregiving spouse with some respite during the day. These programs allow the couple to remain together in their home longer because the "well" spouse gets a break while someone else attends to the one needing care, at least for some period of time. The biggest problem is getting everyone to consider outside help for the first time. This may be the time you will notice rejection of outside help by either the care recipient or caregiver. This should be addressed immediately, with kindness and empathy, but with the understanding that changes will have to be made.

These programs have been developed to provide a safe and secure environment with activities for individuals during the day. This allows family members to get a break from the stress and rigors of full-time caregiving. They can operate in one of two models:

• *Social model:* Services organize themselves to provide socialization and activities that may include exercise, music, special events, and even day trips for their attendees.

Adult day care is particularly appropriate for those whose needs can be met by their own family members.

• *Medical model:* Services are usually staffed by at least one full-time registered nurse who is able to administer medicine and perform routine medical tasks. Most medical models have an affiliation with either a hospital or nursing home. They provide social activities and have on-site physician backup as needed.

Aside from the obvious physical assistance that can be offered through these programs, they may serve as a good source for referrals to other assistance used by the families they help. It is advantageous to have outside professionals who get to know the care recipients and can notify the family of any changes or problems they may observe.

Adult day care is particularly appropriate for those whose needs can be met by their own family members, especially when the family members have to work outside the home during the day but are typically at home evenings and weekends.

Many families at first declare that their mom or dad would never go to such a program. However, it may be the only option that offers enough flexibility for the family to continue to keep a parent at home, rather than having one or both parents forced into a residential facility. Sometimes that can be encouragement enough to try it. Frequently (and often much to the surprise of everyone), Mom and Dad will find that they enjoy getting out of the house and socializing. You may be surprised to learn that Mom and Dad would like a little break from being together 24/7.

• *Meals programs:* Some local senior centers offer community lunches where seniors can also benefit from socialization when they otherwise live alone most of the time. These are called congregate meals. Another option is the Meals on Wheels-type service that provides home-delivered meals for lunch and dinner. Because the volunteers visit the home and get to know the recipients, they become a resource to let family know if there is a problem.

• *Transportation services:* These are usually handicapped-accommodating van services that help seniors get to medical appointments, community centers, and shopping.

• *Emergency response systems:* For people who live alone, these electronic monitors can offer automatic connection to emergency medical or other services when activated. While they are not a replacement for personal contact, they can offer peace of mind when elders have to be left alone for a period of time.

• *Respite care:* Sometimes a caregiver may become ill or indisposed, leaving the care recipient without needed help. Respite care, usually offered at nursing-home, or skilled, facilities, allows the person needing care to stay at a facility while the caregiver is away for an extended time, for a vacation, surgery, or whatever. Advance arrangements can be made. This service can be a lifesaver for both parties. Most facilities will offer some type of respite service if you ask.

The need to give and receive care is a difficult transition for most individuals and families. Loss of independence that comes with aging is a real fear we all share. Some people are naturally better prepared mentally and emotionally for these changes. Stubborn rejection of assistance can cause additional stress for all involved. Now is a good time to have an honest discussion about the available options. By allowing respite for the caregivers, the care recipient may be able to remain in his home longer than could otherwise be possible.

Full-time care: When someone needs full-time care, an important decision must be made about which type of care can best be afforded. Depending on the underlying medical condition, an informal caregiver can still be used—most likely if the caregiver is living with the recipient. When a husband and wife are still together, there is a greater preference for loved ones to remain in their own home for as long as possible. It is important to remember the constant demands that will be placed on the caregiver's time and attention. Even when the kids help on certain weekdays or weekends, the 24/7 commitment can easily become an overwhelming situation for the caregiver. At this juncture, the family should be seeking outside help from formal caregivers. They will be able to quickly determine if the home delivery of care can be managed and then implement a plan to relieve the primary caregiver.

• *Professional home-care programs:* Most people who need care would prefer to receive help and remain in their home. With enough private money or government funding, many people can manage this. Having substantial income or knowledgeable planning can allow this to happen. In my parents' case, when it became obvious that they could not care for themselves alone, we decided to hire formal home care through an agency. I am forever grateful for the care that the aides gave to my parents. Without their help, I could never have given Mom and Dad the life they had together at home in their last years.

Informal caregiving at home is the usual starting place for families. Because I work in the field and had no other family support in the area aside from my mother (who also needed care), I knew we had to hire outside help for Dad. Families will often try to do it themselves. Unfortunately, the ongoing and increasing amount of help that may be needed can become difficult for family members. This is when they either search for a formal care setting or hire outside help.

Professional home-care agencies can provide many types of services that include:

- companionship
- meal preparation and housekeeping
- assistance with bathing, dressing, toileting
- nursing services (dressing changes, injections, wound care)
- rehabilitation services (occupational, physical, speech).

The home may be an ideal environment because the older person can remain with her family and continue to pursue favorite activities. My dad began to write a daily comic strip at the kitchen table when he could no longer walk. The book I made of these cartoons continues to bring joy to many, even though he is no longer here to tell the jokes himself.

Hidden Costs of Home Care

Besides the statistics that I continue to see about the hidden cost of the time spent by informal caregivers looking after their elderly family members, there are other costs to consider.

ome care is usually hard to maintain for an extended period of time when using only informal caregivers.

The necessary supplies and equipment can be expensive. These may include adult diapers, wipes, pads, and hygiene supplies. Home modifications may have to be made, such as ramps and walk-in showers with handrails. Equipment such as walkers, wheelchairs, and commodes will also be required. I can tell you that you will get to know your local home medical-equipment store quite well. Generally, these costs will be paid for out of pocket. Some of the costs may be covered by Medicare if you can get the doctor to write a prescription for necessary equipment or supplies.

When Home Care Might Not Work

Most often when both spouses are alive, they will continue to try to care for each other. As in my parents' case, a wife may risk injury trying to help her husband during a fall or she may simply wear down from the task of caregiving. If children are out of town or unwilling to help (unfortunately this does happen), there may not be anyone to help or even coordinate the necessary services.

Home care is usually hard to maintain for an extended period of time when using only informal caregivers. There is risk to the person in need of care because they may not receive enough help to be safe. Family members are not usually trained to do these tasks, and schedules may not allow people to be there when help is needed.

Furthermore, the individual may not receive adequate social stimulation if left alone a lot of the time. Caregivers get burned out and may not have enough energy or time to spend with their loved ones. If the caregiver can be there only in the morning and after work, the one at home may spend most of his time alone. He may not get any exercise except for getting to the bathroom and back. Many homebound care recipients spend the day sleeping or in front of the television. Malnutrition and dehydration are problems that arise frequently. This is no way to finish a good life.

I remember when we first started home care for my parents. I felt so uncomfortable leaving my father watching television with someone else. That was "my spot" on the couch next to his chair. I felt like someone else was taking my place. I have come to realize that I could never have been there all the time, nor could I have successfully performed the hands-on caregiving work.

There were a number of things necessary to provide adequate home care that I had no idea how to do:

- lift or move someone to avoid injury to both parties

- care for skin properly and prevent bedsores

- deal with incontinence and provide proper sanitation

- maintain personal hygiene

- use devices such as a gait belt or other transfer techniques.

It is one thing to want to do all of this for your parents. Successfully providing the proper care to keep them happy and healthy is something completely different. It was my job to keep the household running. I paid the bills and shopped for food and supplies. I was the person in charge of making sure that aides were there as scheduled and that my parents were well-cared for and happy. However, as the daughter, it was not my job to clean my father when he was soiled, to feed him every meal, or move him from the bed to the chair or to the table for meals. It really takes a team. It was almost another full-time job for me just managing the care that took place in their home.

I cannot stress enough the need for outside information and help if you want to maintain your loved one's safety in their home for the long haul. Short term, most of us can stumble through. In the long term, however, you need to get some help. Having competent advice about available resources may make the difference between successful home care and having to move your loved one into a facility.

Medicaid Home Care Rules

Most people do not want to go to a nursing home to receive the care they need. Community care is unfortunately more complicated to understand because it is offered through a variety of programs with varying levels of care and admission requirements. Community-based Medicaid long-term care services have different eligibility rules, depending on the type of services needed. Most families will need assistance to determine which Medicaid services are available to help with home care and how to maximize their value within the required income and resource levels.

To obtain community-based long-term care, the applicant is currently allowed to keep $14,550 in assets, and she may also retain the home in which she lives. Income over the allowed $829 monthly limit must be spent on medical care. However, she can also pay this monthly excess amount into a *pooled trust* that can be used to pay for other expenses necessary to remain in the community (like property taxes, electricity, and heating bills). If the applicant is a single person, Medicaid will place a lien on the house, to be repaid after his or her death, unless other planning has been done in advance.

The most notable difference between community-based Medicaid services and the more commonly understood nursing-home Medicaid is that there is no look-back required upon application. This can allow many people to access Medicaid services in their home, either because they already have minimal or no assets, or by transferring some assets. This Medicaid planning will be further explored in the next chapter, "Who Will Pay for All of This?"

Long-Term Care Settings Outside of the Home

There are myriad names for the various types of living and care arrangements now available outside the home. Beginning with the lowest level of care provided in the living facility, they basically fall into this order:

• **Senior apartments** *(no care provided):* "Senior-only" apartments are great for people who may want to rent instead of own a home at this stage of their lives. These apartments offer a community with people their own age. For people who are alone and find themselves on a tight budget, this can be a wonderful start in a new place. Many of these communities offer rent subsidies for low-income seniors.

I have many clients who choose this type of living arrangement because it is a simple first step. While it may be simple, it isn't necessarily easy. Many people can't imagine taking apart their household after a long life in the same home. They dread the process of moving. They put it off and leave it to their children to figure out what to do. By making decisions earlier, seniors can have time to enjoy their new life and new friends without the worry of maintaining a home as they get older. The biggest concern with this type of living is that individuals will still have to determine where and how to receive care services when they are needed.

• *Independent living facilities:* These living arrangements are sometimes called *adult homes* or *enriched housing facilities*. These communities are similar to senior apartments, except that they usually offer additional services. They offer group meals and a safe environment. They often provide activities and local transportation. Most adult-care facilities offer private rooms and either private or shared bathrooms, but they are not responsible for the "care needs" of their residents. In many ways these facilities are similar to assisted living, but are not licensed to provide additional care services to help with activities such as bathing, dressing, and transferring. The majority of these facilities do allow for private care aides to be used by their residents. I have helped arrange for care to be brought into this type of apartment setting. Many times, we are able to have the care paid for by a community-based Medicaid program, so that the resident is responsible for only the monthly rent and normal living expenses.

• **_Assisted living:_** These facilities offer medical and personal-care services, as well as housing, meals, and social activities. This can be a big transition for a family member, but may offer the safest and most appropriate setting when care in the home is either unavailable or unsafe. It can also be a great opportunity for a single person to resume a life of her own with other people her own age and relief from the obligations of running a home.

When a person can no longer safely drive or prepare a meal, even home can begin to feel like a prison—especially if he or she is home alone all day and night. I have witnessed many reluctant family members experience pleasantly surprising outcomes after moving to a safe place with good food and company.

Assisted-living arrangements are for those who have some care needs but still want to remain independent. These facilities are licensed and regulated by the state. The services they offer will vary based on these regulations. Typically, they are preferable to a more expensive nursing home for people who need help functioning but don't have the physical, mental, or medical impairments that would require that higher level of care. Residents usually live in their own apartments but have support services available such as:

- assistance with personal care
- up to three meals each day
- 24-hour staff for emergencies and security
- daily activities and entertainment
- housekeeping and laundry services
- help with medication management.

The cost of assisted living can vary depending on the services required by the resident and the amenities offered. Usually, monthly rent includes meals and housekeeping services. Most assisted-living costs are private pay. These facilities are usually covered by long-term care insurance. In addition, if the person qualifies, the VA Aid and Attendance program can offer a pension to help with the costs. Care at this level is typically about half the cost of a skilled-nursing facility.

• *Enhanced assisted living:* These residences must obtain certification proving that they are able to meet the needs of a population that may range from healthy to very physically frail. Residents can be allowed to age in place even when they:

- require more than occasional assistance from medical personnel
- become chair-fast
- chronically require the physical assistance of another person to transfer or walk
- are dependent on medical equipment
- have unmanaged urinary or bowel incontinence.

• *Memory-care residence:* This environment is designed for people with a level of impairment that makes it unsafe for them to continue to stay at home, but who do not require the intensive care of a skilled-nursing facility. Memory care allows a person with memory loss to maintain a level of independence while relying on the safety and security of being in a residential facility with a professional staff. Typically, the residents live in private or semiprivate units and have scheduled activities and programs designed to enhance memory, supervised by trained staff members. The residences are extremely secure, with alarmed or locked areas to ensure no one wanders off. Usually within these secured areas residents can enjoy indoor walking paths, outdoor paths, or gardens.

• *Sub-acute care:* Many times, after a hospital stay (acute care), a person may still have an illness, injury, or disease that has not been fully treated. In my experience, people are being discharged from hospital stays more quickly now and may still require some form of medical care after being released. Technically, this type of treatment is aimed at specific, active, or complex medical conditions, or to administer one or more complex medical treatments not expected to be long term.

Generally, sub-acute care may be needed after acute hospitalization has ended and is usually given in a rehabilitation unit of a nursing facility. This treatment can be community based, but you should consider whether the condition is treatable at home before agreeing to this type of sub-acute care.

• *Nursing homes*: These are also called *skilled-nursing facilities*. For individuals requiring 24-hour care because of the severity or complexity of their nursing needs, a skilled-nursing facility may be the most appropriate setting for them to receive their care. These facilities are sometimes attached to a hospital and offer supervision, necessary therapies, and full-time attention.

Skilled nursing may be needed when family members have chronic physical or mental conditions that require constant supervision or care. This is where many receive the best care after the family can no longer provide safe or continuous care at home.

A skilled-nursing facility offers the highest level of help for elders. This is the most expensive level of care and can be covered by Medicaid when the resident meets the income and resource requirements for the program. It is important to consider that it is the care and not the looks of the facility that will determine your loved one's happiness. Yes, people in a nursing home are sometimes called patients and they may sleep in hospital beds. These facilities often charge daily flat rates like hospitals, based on private or semiprivate rooms. However, even though the facilities may look cold and clinical, it is often in the individual's best interest to be there.

• *Continuing-care retirement communities* (CCRC): These unique facilities are designed to allow seniors to enter the community under a contract that will provide higher levels of care, as needed, all within the same complex for an agreed-upon fee. These facilities are also called life-care communities. This living arrangement can be a great idea for couples who have not purchased long-term care insurance but still want to limit how much they will ultimately pay—no matter how their needs change. It is also especially attractive for people whose children live far away.

I have many happy clients in continuing-care communities. They have now eliminated the worries associated with deciding where and how they will get and afford the care they need, when they need it. Otherwise, Mom or Dad might have had to consider moving when their needs changed. In a CCRC, this is an easy transition within the same community, for the same cost. For people with no family in the area, this can provide great peace of mind.

There is usually a sizable down payment required ($200,000 to $400,000) that is sometimes paid for by the sale of the old family residence. Often, a percentage of this down payment (up to 90 percent) is returned to the family after the death of the second spouse. Monthly fees ($2,000 to $4,000) cover all amenities and may increase with inflation over time. However, the monthly fee does not increase when one or both spouses require higher levels of care, like assisted living or skilled nursing.

You have to be in good health and able to live independently when you enter. The qualifying requirements are usually less strict than those for purchasing private long-term care insurance. This makes it easier for people who have started planning later in life to still control how much they will spend on their care.

• *Multi-level communities:* More of these campus-type facilities are being created all the time. They provide independent housing, assisted living, and nursing-home services all within close proximity or even in connected facilities. Each level is paid for on its own, so there is no large entrance fee. As the care needs of one or both spouses increase, they can still remain in close proximity to each other. However, by the time both family members require higher levels of care, costs can become quite high. Medicaid can eventually pay for nursing-home costs, but assisted living will still most likely be private pay. Most families will need to plan to be able to manage several levels of care at the same time.

6

WHO WILL PAY
FOR ALL OF THIS?

HE GOOD NEWS is that care costs may not be overwhelming at first. Many people need only minimal help at the beginning. Care needs then typically increase as their condition declines. This can give the family some time to plan, at first using the senior's income to supplement family help with paid caregivers, as needed.

Furthermore, new and creative ways are constantly being developed to help elders obtain the care they need, either in their home or in a facility. As covered in the last chapter, there are numerous levels of care that may be able to address an individual's needs for an extended period of time before he needs nursing-home care.

Sometimes, however, a major event like a stroke or a serious fall can immediately force someone to need skilled or full-time care. The bad news is that skilled care currently costs approximately $425 per day in some areas. That works out to nearly $130,000 each year.

This chapter will cover the major funding sources for each level of care. To make the best decisions about paying for long-term care, you will need to know:

- the cost of services at each level of care
- what private funds you have available to pay for care
- which public programs you might be eligible for and what they cover; each program will have its own eligibility requirements and cover different services.

After the age of 65, most seniors are covered under Medicare as their primary health insurer. Many also have a supplemental policy to pay for expenses not covered by Medicare. What many people don't realize is that Medicare and their private insurance will not pay for long-term care for an extended period of time. Medicare does not cover the cost of nursing care after 100 days. Furthermore, payment will stop as soon as it is determined that the care needed is *custodial*—such as help with bathing, dressing, eating—and not *skilled*.

For example, after a hospitalization, a person may need rehabilitation to regain her ability to live independently at home. The care required to help her will be paid for by Medicare, but only for a limited amount of time. Most private health insurances, including health maintenance organizations and managed care, follow rules very similar to Medicare. If services are covered, they are generally for short-term, skilled, medically necessary care.

Because of the limited coverage provided by traditional insurance sources used by most seniors (i.e., Medicare and traditional health insurance) and the financial impoverishment requirements of Medicaid, most families are required to privately pay for a significant portion of their long-term care costs—at least at the beginning. The rest of this chapter will hopefully make this more clear.

Medicare long-term care: Medicare will help pay for a short period of time if you are in a skilled-nursing facility or for some initial home health care, but only after you have been admitted to a hospital and have stayed for at least three days. Furthermore, you must be admitted to a nursing facility within 30 days of this hospital stay or require skilled services at home, such as nursing or other therapy. If you meet these conditions, Medicare will pay for some of your costs for up to 100 days (about three months).

Medicare pays in full for the first 20 days. You then have a co-pay of $140 per day (the current amount for 2014) for days 21 through 100. In most cases, you will have to privately pay for 100 percent of the cost for each day that you stay in a skilled-nursing facility or require skilled services at home beyond day 100.

Medicare will not pay nursing-home costs for someone who is admitted directly to a facility from their home.

Some of my clients have been told recently that Medicare will not pay for their nursing-home costs because they had not been formally admitted to a hospital for the treatment they received. Whatever the reason, some hospitals and doctors have been treating people under *observation status,* which fails to qualify

*It is important to have some money available
to be attractive to a facility of your choice.*

them for Medicare coverage. Recently implemented regulations require immediate notification that the patient's services will not be covered by Medicare under such circumstances.

You can (and should) appeal the categorization of observation status. Otherwise you may be forced to pay for all of the skilled services at rehabilitation beginning on day one. News stories have begun to bring to light this disturbing trend. Hopefully the practice will be stopped. For now, it is forcing patients to pay for services that would otherwise be covered by Medicare.

Private health insurance: Supplemental health-care insurance will usually cover the co-pays for your hospitalization and nursing-home care. However, it does not usually pay for services not approved by Medicare. You should always check with your private insurance carrier in case you have a special plan that might cover payment, but this is not typically the case.

Self-payment: There is a good reason that nursing homes and assisted-living facilities require a list of assets from families before they will admit them for rehabilitation services—Medicare will pay only for a short period of time, as described above. The facilities know this. After Medicare ceases payment, families are faced with significant out-of-pocket costs. Money will have to be available to pay these bills, or an application for Medicaid will have to be made as quickly as possible. That is also why facilities ask about any gifts that have been made within the past five years. These gifts will cause a problem with Medicaid coverage unless some action is taken to return the gifts, as I explain later.

People always want to know if there is a certain amount of money you should have to be "attractive" to a nursing home. I cannot say that there is any such number. I can tell you that the selection process does depend in large part on how long someone will be able to privately pay for his or her care. The government reimburses facilities for the cost of care provided to residents approved for Medicaid. But that reimbursement is much lower than what they can charge for residents who pay with their own funds. Most people will run out of private funds sooner or later, but the facility would rather have that happen later—in every case!

It is important to have some money available to be attractive to a facility of your choice. Unfortunately, in the current system, this entire process usually takes place very quickly and without a lot of information or assistance. Hospitals employ *discharge planners* to move patients out of the hospital to their home or a rehabilitation facility. In most cases, families are asked to complete a form listing everything they own and any transfers of assets made within the past five years. Then they are given a list of facilities from which to make their choices.

The discharge planner will make phone calls and determine a facility that will accept your loved one. It is that impersonal. Many factors go into a facility's decision to accept a resident or not. As I said, the ability to pay privately is part of the determination. But other factors include the type and amount of care that will be required by the patient and the availability of beds in the facility. Sometimes knowing someone influential can help, but it is usually just the best fit the discharge planner can find at the time.

If you will be privately paying for some time, you may be able to move to a different facility if you do not like where you have been placed. I would highly recommend using the services of a geriatric-care manager to make sure your loved one is in the best possible facility for his or her specific needs.

Long-term care insurance: This insurance can be one of the greatest purchases you ever make. It can help protect your assets from being depleted when paying for the extremely high costs of long-term care. However, it is not right for everyone. If your assets are not far above the levels required for Medicaid coverage, you probably don't need to insure against the costs you will be expected to pay. We usually tell couples that they should have at least $300,000 to $700,000 of countable assets, not including their primary residence, before considering the purchase of long-term care insurance. In addition, if the purchase is going to affect your current lifestyle and cut into your current living expenses, you probably don't need it.

The peace of mind that comes from having a good policy to pay for the type of care you want, at the facility of your choosing, can be very attractive. However, you need to know about the type of policy you will be purchasing and what it will, and will not, do for you. It can be very expensive to purchase this type of insurance later in life. You also have to be healthy enough to qualify for it. Most states regulate long-term care insurance and set strict regulations on minimum standards to protect consumers.

There are some basic benefits that should be part of any policy you purchase, including:

- home-care and nursing-home care coverage
- assisted-living benefits
- enough daily coverage to pay for most of the current cost of care in your area
- short elimination periods (number of days you are required to privately pay before the policy kicks in—fewer are better)
- a guarantee that the policy is renewable
- a guarantee that the premium will be waived when you start receiving benefits
- inflation protection (usually 5 percent compounded).

You should also identify how long the policy will pay (three years, five years, or lifetime).

Long-term care insurance can be expensive, but so is the cost of long-term care services. Ask anyone who has had to pay privately for any extended period of time. If you have enough money to be contemplating an inheritance for your children, you need to protect the money you want to leave them from being depleted in the last years of your life.

When you buy long-term care insurance, you will be purchasing a contract from an insurance company. It will pay for certain types of coverage under certain conditions. The problem

If you never want to be cared for in a nursing home, why would you buy a policy that pays for nursing-home coverage?

is trying to determine what you might need in the future. None of us has a crystal ball. However, there are some things you need to consider among the many options that will be offered. If you are going to spend the money on a policy, you should buy one that will work for you when you need it.

• If you never want to be cared for in a nursing home and you are serious about that, why would you buy a policy that pays for nursing-home coverage? You may be able to purchase a really good policy that covers only assisted living and home care. You can then do other planning to protect most of your other assets from nursing-home costs and apply for Medicaid to cover them should the worst occur.

• If you don't have unlimited funds to pay for a policy, you might want to purchase five years of coverage. That amount of time will allow you or your family to do other types of planning. If you transfer assets at that time, you would currently have enough coverage to get you past any look-back period that may apply to the transfer. (Medicaid planning is in the next chapter.) As you will see, if you apply for Medicaid after the five-year look-back period has passed, you may qualify for Medicaid coverage of your nursing-home costs.

• Make sure the policy has a home-care option. Medicaid's home-care options will be discussed later, but home care under Medicaid is much more difficult to arrange. If it cannot be done, some people end up in a nursing home before they might have to, just to get the costs paid. If you have home-care coverage, you may never have to see a nursing home, as most people prefer.

• Make sure you compare several companies' options and rates. Also, make sure you purchase a policy from a highly rated insurance company. Many companies entered the field of long-term care insurance only to find out they weren't prepared for the high costs as claims were made. The field of companies now offering long-term care insurance has narrowed; you should be able to select from three or four good companies. Make sure you are comparing apples to apples and look at similar coverage options from each company. This is why it is probably best to purchase from an independent insurance agent who is qualified to show you products from several companies at once.

• Be honest on your application and make sure the company "underwrites" you at the time of purchase. You want to be sure the company agrees to pay for your care based on your current health and that there will not be questions about your initial qualification for coverage when you need the policy later.

• If you are a couple, you may be able to buy a *shared-care policy* covering both of you for less. You would buy a pool of benefits that can be split between you and your spouse.

107

• Again, you want to choose an insurance agent who represents a number of companies so that you can compare policies. Try to find an agent who has been trained and who is designated as *Certified in Long-Term Care (CLTC)*, an independent professional certification.

State partnership policies: States have created a public/private partnership between their department of health (Medicaid) and the insurance industry. If you purchase a state partnership policy, you will use the insurance proceeds, supplemented by your own assets and income, for a certain number of years (e.g., three or six), and then you will automatically qualify for Medicaid in that state. Generally, you will be able to keep an unlimited amount of assets and still qualify for Medicaid. Your income, however, will continue to be available and must be "spent down" to Medicaid levels. This is a point that is rarely adequately explained by insurance agents. If you have a large pension that will pay for the rest of your life or large retirement assets, the amount of income that you have to spend on care each month may defeat the purpose of owning this type of insurance. These policies should be reviewed with your elder law attorney and financial consultant before purchasing, specifically because of the income spend-down requirement.

Innovative products: In the last few years, some insurance companies have created hybrid insurance products that may be more attractive to some people. They offer features of both life insurance and long-term care insurance. They guarantee a *death benefit* if the long-term care coverage is not used. The amount used if coverage is needed is subtracted from the ultimate death benefit.

This takes away some people's concerns that they may pay for a policy and never use it.

Medicaid: Medicaid is the federal/state program that many people rely on to pay their long-term care costs. It is often confused with Medicare, a federal program administered uniformly across the country. Medicare is an *entitlement program,* meaning that everyone who reaches age 65 and receives Social Security benefits also receives Medicare.

In contrast, Medicaid is a joint federal/state program that helps people with low income and few assets pay for medical care and long-term care services. Medicaid eligibility requires that you be considered *impoverished* by its guidelines. Federal requirements determine who can be eligible for Medicaid and what services are covered. While each state administers its own Medicaid program, states must conform to federal guidelines to receive federal assistance. States, however, have considerable leeway in how they operate the program.

Medicaid is designed to be the *payer of last resort.* To qualify, you must meet financial and other eligibility rules. In addition, these rules differ by state. To complicate things further, both federal and state governments are continually changing eligibility rules and restrictions. Most recently, the *Deficit Reduction Act of 2005* (DRA) significantly changed the rules for transferring assets for nursing-home Medicaid. Unlike Medicare, Medicaid does pay for custodial care in nursing homes and at home.

Medicaid long-term care: To qualify for Medicaid long-term care services, you must meet a minimum level of care needed, as

To qualify for Medicaid long-term care services,
both income and assets tests are applied.

determined by a nursing assessment. The need for skilled-nursing care is an automatic qualification. To receive Medicaid services at home or in another community setting, you usually have to meet nursing-home eligibility standards.

Income and asset requirements: To qualify for Medicaid long-term care services, both income and assets tests are applied.

Income: When Medicaid pays for nursing-home care, residents are allowed to keep only a small personal-needs allowance of $50 per month. This can be used to pay for things not covered by Medicaid like clothing or telephone service. For a single person, the rest of his income must be applied toward the cost of care.

If you have a *community spouse* (one who stays at home while you are receiving services), he or she will be allowed to keep a *minimum monthly maintenance needs allowance (MMMNA)*. This allowance is made to avoid impoverishing the healthy spouse. States set their own limits for the spousal allowance, with the highest amount currently at $2,931 per month. If the community spouse's own income is below this amount, the shortfall can be made up from the nursing-home spouse's income above the allowance.

In some cases, it is also possible to argue for an increased resource allowance for the community spouse, if the combined income is below the allowable amount. This increase will require a fair hearing to prove that income from earnings on the additional resources are required to raise the community spouse's income to the MMMNA.

Assets: Medicaid will pay for nursing-home services if the applicant has resources at or below an amount determined by each state. Resources are basically anything that can be converted to cash to pay for care. Resource limits set by states currently range from $2,000 to $14,400 for an individual applicant. Resources include all types of assets, such as:

- checking and savings accounts
- investment assets
- vacation homes
- contents of your safe-deposit box
- cash values of life insurance policies.

If there is a spouse who remains in the community when the other becomes a resident of the nursing home, the spouse may keep one-half of the couple's resources, up to a maximum amount determined by the value of the couple's available resources. This amount is limited by minimums and maximums set by each state. Currently, the minimum resource allowance for a community spouse ranges from $21,000 to $74,820. The 2014 maximum allowance is $117,240. The community spouse is also allowed to keep the family residence, up to an *equity value,* or fair-market value, determined by the state. For example, New York currently exempts a residence with equity value below $814,000.

Medicaid: *How You Qualify for Long-Term Care*

Before Medicaid will pay for your long-term care, you must prove that your total assets are below the "allowance" amount. You also need to disclose what you have given away within the past five years—a penalty will be assessed for those transfers. There is also an income limit over which you must contribute some of your monthly income toward the cost of the care.

ASSETS YOU CAN KEEP

IF YOU ARE MARRIED
(spouse remains at home):
- primary residence *(up to a value determined by each state)*
- one car of any value
- IRAs, if in "payout status" *(taking required minimum distributions, payments are considered income—see below)**
- community spouse resource allowance *(varies by state; ranges from a minimum of $21,000 to $74,820; a maximum of $117,240)*
- Medicaid applicant resource allowance *(varies by state; from $2,000 to $14,550)*

IF YOU ARE SINGLE:
- one car, if used for medical appointments
- IRA, if in "payout status" *(taking required minimum distributions, which are considered income—see below)**
- Medicaid applicant resource allowance *(varies by state; from $2,000 to $14,550)*

*Beyond what's listed above, **you must "spend down" the following to qualify:***
ALL OF YOUR ASSETS, *including:*

- investments
- bank accounts
- other real property *(vacation homes)*
- cash value of life insurance *(anything that can be converted to cash)*

***You also will be penalized for any* GIFT TRANSFERS** *during the past 60 months; the total value of these transfers will be added back:*
- money to family or friends
- properties sold at less than fair-market value

MONTHLY INCOME YOU CAN KEEP

SPOUSE REMAINING AT HOME:
- $2,931 maximum allowance
1/4 of spouse's income above $2,931 must be paid to nursing home.

APPLICANT:
- $50

*Otherwise, all income must go toward **your monthly nursing-home costs,** including:*
- Social Security
- pensions
- rental income
- required minimum distributions from IRAs*

Without other planning, assets and income above these levels must be spent down on care or other exempt resources before Medicaid will begin to pay. These exempt resources include:

- personal possessions, including clothing and jewelry
- one car for the community spouse, and a second car if it is used as transportation for the resident
- prepaid funerals for the applicant and spouse; their children and spouses; their brothers, sisters, and their spouses; and even parents
- income-producing property or property used in a trade or business
- assets that are for some reason otherwise unavailable (for example, a family camp that is owned with distant family members who will not sell the property).

Transfers of Assets

Nearly every day, older clients ask how much money they can give to their children and still have Medicaid pay for their care. Like most lawyers, I answer, "it depends." You can imagine that Medicaid doesn't want you to give all of your money away and then ask them to pay for your expensive nursing-home care. But to make sure, the Deficit Reduction Act of 2005 made the asset transfer restrictions more complicated and severe.

What is considered a transfer? No, you cannot give $14,000 to each of your children each year, as allowed under the IRS gift-tax rules, if you want to be covered by Medicaid. We are dealing with the government agency responsible for paying for the care of those who cannot pay for it themselves. Medicaid rules allow for certain transfer exceptions between spouses and to disabled children. However, generally speaking, no gifting is allowed within five years of applying for Medicaid nursing-home care.

As explained later, community-based or home-care Medicaid operates under different regulations that do not require a review of all transactions during a look-back period. This leaves the possibility of transferring assets and qualifying for community-based Medicaid programs right away. Unfortunately, qualifying for Medicaid-covered home care can be a lengthy process. Many cannot afford to pay privately until they are accepted into the program.

How Is the Penalty Calculated?

All transfers made within the look-back period are added together and divided by the average Medicaid nursing-home cost in your area. Each year states publish local averages, by region, which give us the monthly number. In Western New York, for example, the current monthly rate is $8,971. Therefore, if several transfers were made within the look-back period that totaled $8,971, the result would be a one-month penalty that Medicaid would not pay.

Medicaid will ask for all financial records, statements, and tax returns for the last 60 months and thoroughly review all monies coming in and going out to find any uncompensated transfers. Those transfers will be added up and divided by the monthly rate to determine the penalty. There is no cap on the length of the penalty period that can be imposed. As a result, it is important to know how much has been transferred during the 60-month look-back period. If the amount will calculate to a penalty longer than 60 months, you should wait until the look-back has expired before applying for Medicaid benefits.

People always want to know if there is a "secret amount" they can give away that won't be counted as a transfer. "Can't I give my kids $1,000 each for Christmas?" I have to answer that it is the decision of each Medicaid examiner to decide what will be penalized. Remember, we are asking that the government begin paying for care that can cost more than $11,000 each month. The workers take their jobs seriously. The rules have been established to ensure that truly needy people qualify. Have you always given your children $1,000 for Christmas? Or have you suddenly become generous now that you may have to use your money to pay for long-term care?

When Does the Penalty Begin?

The Deficit Reduction Act also changed when the penalty period begins. Under current law, the penalty does not begin until:

- the person who made the transfer has entered a nursing home
- he or she has applied for Medicaid
- he or she would otherwise qualify for Medicaid, except for the transfer.

This change has caused hardship for both residents and nursing homes. That is why nursing homes are increasingly stringent in their review of assets and transfers before they will accept patients, even for rehabilitation after a hospital stay.

Some Transfers Are Allowed

While most transfers made within 60 months before applying will count toward the penalty, some transfers are allowed. These transfers can be made even after you have moved to a nursing home:

- transfers between spouses
- transfers to a blind or permanently disabled child
- transfer of your house (but not other assets) to a child who has lived with you for two years before you entered the nursing home, or to a sibling who already owns part of the house and who has lived with you for at least one year.

Let's look at an example: Mary lives in Western New York, where the monthly cost for nursing-home care is calculated by Medicaid to be $8,971. She transfers $89,710 to her children on Nov. 1, 2013, and has to move into a nursing home on Nov. 1, 2014. She privately pays for her care and spends down to Medicaid eligibility (currently $14,500) by Nov. 1, 2015. She applies for Medicaid. The Department of Social Services will determine that she would be eligible for Medicaid, except for the transfer she made in 2013. Therefore, it will impose a 10-month period of ineligibility because of the transfer.

The facility may look to Mary's family to give the money back when Medicaid denies her application. It would be surprising that the facility accepted Mary in the first place, had her family truthfully disclosed the transfers. If they had not disclosed the transfers, the nursing home could have legal recourse against the family.

Special Asset Categories for Medicaid Eligibility

• *Annuities:* Many of my clients have purchased annuities in recent years because they offered a better interest rate than CDs

Generally speaking, no gifting is allowed within five years of applying for Medicaid nursing-home care.

at the time. Unfortunately, most people do not understand the complex rules that govern most annuity contracts. The government took note of certain "balloon payment" annuities being used to shield assets. In response, it created special rules for assets held under the terms of an annuity contract.

An *immediate annuity* is a contract with an insurance company under which the consumer pays an amount to the company up front; the company then sends the consumer a monthly check for a specific period of time, or for the rest of his or her life. By this process, use of an annuity can convert an asset into an income stream. However, Medicaid has rigid guidelines for determining whether an annuity will be treated as an income stream instead of an asset. It must be: irrevocable (the annuitant cannot take funds out of the annuity except for the monthly payments); non-transferable; and actuarially sound—the payment period cannot be longer than the annuitant's life expectancy and the total of the anticipated payments have to equal the cost of the annuity.

The Department of Social Services has additional requirements for annuities. The DSS must be named a beneficiary of the annuity up to the amount of Medicaid benefits paid on behalf of the Medicaid recipient. If the Medicaid recipient has a spouse or disabled child, DSS must be named as a secondary beneficiary. If the applicant does not disclose enough information about the annuity, DSS can deny or terminate coverage for long-term care services.

As you can see, depending upon the assets held by a Medicaid applicant, the process of determining available assets and income can become quite complex. You can read this book and many others related to Medicaid rules in an attempt to learn how the process will work. However, the application process is complex, even if you do not have a complicated case. Applications should be reviewed or submitted by a knowledgeable professional.

• *Retirement accounts:* As mentioned earlier, retirement accounts are treated differently as an asset category when calculating your resources for Medicaid eligibility. These include IRAs and qualified retirement accounts like a 403(b) or other work-related pension plans. This analysis can be tricky. Some people do not know which of their investment accounts may have started out as retirement plans and have since been re-invested in annuities or other types of accounts. They may not be easily recognized as "retirement" monies on their statements. Brokers and other investment professionals will use the term "qualified" when referring to these accounts.

Retirement assets are considered a source of pension income and therefore may not be counted as a resource. They may be calculated into the "income" portion of your application. However, for that to happen, the applicant and spouse must be receiving annual periodic payments. This happens automatically at age 70½ when you have to begin taking the required minimum distributions from the account. If your spouse is not yet 70½ and you want to preserve the asset, he or she can apply to begin receiving periodic payments even before the required age.

If you are single, the Department of Social Services has its own table to determine the monthly distribution from your retirement account that must be used. This table requires a larger distribution than that required by the Internal Revenue Service and is based on the life expectancy of the applicant. If you have a spouse, the distribution amounts for both of you will continue to be determined by the IRS tables.

• *Jointly held assets*: For financial accounts, all assets held in joint name with another party will be presumed to be owned by the Medicaid applicant. For savings and checking accounts held in the names of both spouses, amounts over the applicant's allowance ($14,500) can be transferred into the name of the community spouse. Many older individuals name their children as joint owners on their bank accounts. This is fine to do, but the entire account will be considered as an asset "owned" by the Medicaid applicant. This is a presumption that can be rebutted if, in fact, the funds were not originally owned by the applicant.

Some people own property jointly with a brother or sister. This is usually because they inherited it from their parents. The property will have to be sold, if it can be divided. The Medicaid worker will have to be satisfied that the sibling will not allow the property to be sold for it not to be considered an available resource.

• *Trusts:* Whether or not assets held in a trust are included when determining Medicaid eligibility will depend on the terms of the trust. It really depends on whether the applicant can have access to the funds held in the trust. For example, assets held in a revocable or living trust can always be taken out by the person who set it up. Consequently, they will be included when determining available resources. If the applicant or spouse created an irrevocable trust from which payments of principal cannot be made to him or her, then the assets will not be counted. However, the transfer of assets into an irrevocable trust during the look-back period will cause a penalty. If income distributions can be made from the trust to the grantor, then the income from the trust will be considered available when applying for Medicaid.

• *Primary residence:* If you are single and need to be in a nursing home to receive care, your home will be considered an available resource for purposes of Medicaid eligibility. You can submit a form called intent to return home and the value will not be used in your eligibility calculation. However, a lien will be placed on the house to be paid back upon sale, up to the amount of benefits supplied by the government to pay for your care.

If you have a spouse who will remain in the home while you are in the nursing facility, the house is considered an exempt resource for the community spouse and will not be counted. In a nutshell, unless you can find a suitable mate after the death of your spouse, you should probably consider doing some type of planning to protect the equity in your home in the event you need skilled-nursing care in the future! We will discuss planning alternatives in the next chapter.

As mentioned before, you can also transfer the house to a caregiver child or sibling who has lived with you and is part owner of the property. As you can see, if you are considering moving assets as a plan to receive Medicaid benefits, transfers should be made carefully, considering the consequences involved. In reality, you shouldn't be making transfers without competent advice from an experienced elder law attorney. In addition, your attorney should be consulting with your financial planner to ensure your overall financial picture is considered. Most people have worked long and hard to accumulate the savings that remain as they get older.

It is a natural tendency to want to give money to your children rather than spend it on a nursing home. But this is not the time to be listening to your children or friends at the senior center about how to best accomplish your goal. The rules are complicated and transfers have consequences. You have to consider the income and capital gains tax problems you could create by outright gifts to your children.

In addition, your children may not be in a position to "hold" assets for you because you may have grandchildren in need of financial aid for college at the same time or they might not be financially stable themselves. However well-intentioned they may be, children holding assets "outright" for their parents can cause a lot of heartache. The child could have an accident and be sued.

For example, an older man left his life insurance to his son upon his death. He had told him to "hold it" for his wife and to use it for her benefit. Now they are in my office because the son will only begrudgingly give his mother spending money and she feels hurt. In this case, the father could have left the money in a trust that told the son exactly what the father intended.

Veterans Benefits

Veterans benefits can play a crucial role in planning for long-term care needs. Many veterans or surviving spouses of veterans are unaware that they could likely qualify for significant cash benefits (up to $30,480 annually) under the Aid and Attendance pension.

This pension provides benefits for veterans and their surviving spouses who require the help of another person to assist in ADLs, the basic activities of daily living (eating, dressing, bathing, toileting, transferring). The care received in an assisted-living facility also qualifies. That is where I see this benefit used most often.

Your physician must establish that you need daily assistance. You do not have to require assistance with all of the activities listed above; you just need to show that you cannot function completely on your own. Currently, the pension can provide up to $1,758 per month to a veteran, $1,130 per month to a surviving spouse, or $2,085 per month to a couple. A veteran can apply for his or her sick spouse if the spouse's medical expenses deplete their combined monthly income, and receive up to $1,380.

Increased pension payments are based on the need for aid and attendance, meaning "permanently and totally disabled as to render them utterly helpless, or so nearly so as to require the constant personal aid and attendance of another person."

Requirements

• *Active service:* The first requirement for a Veterans Affairs pension benefit eligibility is that the veteran must have completed at least 90 days of active military, naval, or air service, with at least one day of the 90 during a qualifying wartime period. The types of service that meet this requirement are relatively broad.

The qualifying wartime period requirement is fairly straightforward, with little room for interpretation. At least one day of the veteran's active service must be within a defined period of war. Periods of war applicable to today's veterans include:

- World War II *(Dec. 7, 1941 – Dec. 31, 1946)*
- Korean conflict *(June 27, 1950 – Jan. 31, 1955)*
- Vietnam era *(Feb. 28, 1961 – May 7, 1975, for veterans who served in the Republic of Vietnam during that period; otherwise Aug. 5, 1964 – May 7, 1975)*
- Persian Gulf era *(Aug. 2, 1990, through a future date to be set by law or presidential proclamation).*

• *Not dishonorably discharged:* To qualify as a veteran, a person must have been discharged under "conditions other than dishonorable." A form called a DD-214 has been issued to military members upon separation from active service since 1950. Various forms were used before that as "discharge papers." Any of these forms will prove the required service for application purposes.

• *Need for aid and attendance:* After establishing the requisite military service, the claimant must demonstrate the need for regular "aid and attendance of another person" in order to receive the enhanced monthly pension. This assistance must be regular, but need not be constant. The need for aid and attendance is defined as "helplessness or being so nearly helpless as to require the regular aid and attendance of another person."

The Veterans Benefits Administration uses several factors to determine the need for regular aid and attendance. A claimant need not prove each of them—the administration assesses his condition as a whole. The factors include whether the claimant can:

- dress or undress by himself

- keep himself neat and presentable

- adjust a prosthetic device (that needs frequent adjustment) without assistance

- feed himself (due to loss of coordination or weakness)

- toilet by himself or herself

- protect himself from any dangers of his daily environment.

A claimant must show a need for assistance from another person and must provide evidence that the assistance is currently being received. You cannot just provide information that the veteran requires daily assistance. This does not prove a need for regular aid and attendance. To be approved, you should submit a physician's affidavit indicating need, as well as evidence of actual assistance (like an invoice from a home health agency showing that the services were actually provided).

• *Permanent and total disability:* An eligible claimant must prove that he or she is permanently and totally disabled, or is simply over the age of 65. If a veteran's permanent and total disability was service-connected, he may qualify for disability compensation and non-service-connected pension benefits. However, duplication of benefits is not allowed and you will have to decide on either compensation or pension payments. It is important to know that you will not automatically receive the higher benefit amount—you must select between the two programs.

• *Limited assets and income:* The VA will not award a pension if the claimant's assets are reasonably sufficient to provide for his or her maintenance. Generally, you cannot receive a pension benefit if your countable assets exceed $80,000.

Assets: The VA evaluates net worth by determining whether the claimant's assets—without the VA pension—are adequate to meet his or her basic needs for a reasonable period of time. In determining whether a claimant's assets prohibit pension eligibility, the VA considers life expectancy, countable income, number of dependents, potential rate of depletion, liquidity of the assets, and unusual medical expenses. The $80,000 limit on a claimant's assets is not a strict rule, but rather a guideline. As an example, a 65-year-old veteran with an $80,000 estate and $20,000 in annual medical expenses could be approved, while a 90-year-old with the same size estate could be denied due to excessive net worth.

The takeaway here is that there is really no hard and fast rule that determines a claimant's eligibility based on her net worth—the key is whether a claimant can reasonably utilize her assets to meet her needs without VA assistance.

• The VA determines available resources differently than the Medicaid system. In general, the calculation is not as strict.

• Assets of both spouses are counted in the calculation. Some assets are specifically excluded from the net-worth calculation, such as the primary residence.

• The VA also considers whether an asset can be easily converted into cash. For example, say the veteran owns a lot with an assessed value of $50,000, but property values in the area have dropped substantially recently. If he can show that he is unlikely to receive more than $10,000 if he sold the property, then the VA would value it at $10,000.

• Jointly owned assets are counted only to the extent of the veteran's ownership share. For example, assume a veteran purchases a $10,000 certificate of deposit, and then adds his daughter as joint owner. The VA's policy is to consider $5,000 as available to the veteran. This means planning can be done to make a veteran eligible for VA benefits, even after he is receiving care. But this planning should be done within the context of understanding that Medicaid and its rules may come into play within the next five years.

Income: An otherwise-eligible veteran must also meet income guidelines to be entitled to VA pension benefits. A veteran's income for VA purposes is determined by subtracting unreimbursed medical expenses from his gross income. Gross income includes all interest income from investments. In addition, if the claimant owns a tax-deferred retirement account, such as an IRA, any distribution from that account must be counted as income. The VA requires inclusion of the entire distribution as income, even though it includes a partial return of principal.

When a veteran and spouse are joint owners of an income-producing asset, each spouse must include his or her portion of the income on the application form, since income from each spouse is countable. If a veteran owns a joint account with someone who isn't his spouse, only his prorated share of the income is included. The veteran's unreimbursed medical expenses are then deducted.

Treatment of trusts: Do assets held in a trust count as assets or income for VA purposes? Basically, whether assets or income are counted depends upon whether the veteran receives benefit from those funds. The VA follows a three-part rule to determine this:

- actual ownership
- such control over the property that the claimant may direct it to be used for the claimant's benefit
- actual allocation of the funds for the claimant's benefit.

Because there is no look-back period for the disposition of assets, an irrevocable trust can be used to reduce a person's net worth and allow her to become eligible for benefits. For the assets of the irrevocable trust to be excluded, the trustee cannot be allowed to distribute any of the income or principal back to the veteran.

Spousal and dependent eligibility: Pensions for non-service-connected disabilities are either categorized as *live pensions* or *death pensions.* Live pensions are those where a veteran is claiming pension benefits based on his or her own service, while eligibility for death pensions arises after the veteran is deceased.

Surviving spouses and dependents are eligible to apply for death pension benefits.

A surviving spouse must have been married to the veteran for at least one year and they must have lived together continuously from the time of marriage until the veteran's death. In addition, the surviving spouse must not have remarried since the veteran's death. It is important to plan for Aid and Attendance pension benefits within the context of a comprehensive long-term care plan. If it is likely that a client will need long-term care in the foreseeable future, and also likely that he or she could qualify for Medicaid payments, you have to be very careful when transferring assets to qualify for VA pension benefits. These transfers are currently not "seen" on an application. But if you need to go to a nursing home within five years of making those transfers, a penalty will be assessed if you apply for Medicaid.

Further, the VA reduces pension benefits to $90 per month for Medicaid recipients residing in long-term care facilities. One exception to this reduction occurs when the veteran's spouse receives long-term care through Medicaid while the veteran remains in the community. While the veteran would continue to receive his or her pension, such payments would count as non-exempt unearned income in most states.

I have to include a warning here ...

As I write this, Congress just failed to pass the *Veterans Pension Protection Act,* which was intended to "fix" the current backlog of veterans benefit claims. This act also included a penalty period for the Aid and Attendance benefit. If the bill had passed, the VA would have imposed a three-year rule denying benefits equal to assets transferred during that period. While the transfer penalty may have been avoided for now, the issue is not dead and will most likely be proposed again in the near future.

The next chapter will explain some ways you can plan to pay for care, using your assets in combination with programs we have just described.

7

HOW CAN YOU PLAN
FOR LONG-TERM CARE?

HEN MY HUSBAND, an emergency room physician, told me that "TMB" was my father's diagnosis, I had never heard of such a thing. Dad was 93 and having problems with his balance. We had tested everything we could think of and nothing showed up as an exact cause or something for which there was a treatment.

As he explained, my father's body was slowing down and so were all the connections and communications between his brain and his legs. He said my dad had TMB: *Too many birthdays!*

At some point we may all need help because our body can't do what it used to do. If you live long enough to be diagnosed with TMB, you may need outside help to receive the care you need. When you need care that can't be provided by informal

Private pay for long-term care can become prohibitively expensive as more and more hours are required.

caregivers alone, you have to pay for "formal" care to help in some way. The plan may be to start with some assistance where caregivers can come into the home to help. As you will remember, traditional Medicare and private insurance usually will not pay for much, nor for an extended period of time. Private pay can be manageable for a while, but it can become prohibitively expensive as more and more hours are required. Unless you have long-term care insurance, you will be likely be looking for help from one or more assistance programs like Medicaid or those through the Veterans Affairs Department.

Both the VA Aid and Attendance program and Medicaid require applicants to prove "need" by meeting required asset and income thresholds. For both programs, applicants must prove that they are unable to pay for the required care. Legal strategies have been developed to allow participation in these programs by transferring assets out of the ownership and control of the applicant. While I mentioned this briefly in previous chapters, this chapter will explain some of the strategies in more detail.

Asset Preservation Is a Personal Decision

For most people, the high cost of long-term care services comes as an unexpected shock to their financial plans. Most of us cannot afford to pay in excess of $100,000 per year for an extended time without running out of money. Alternative payment sources like Medicaid will not be available until assets have been spent down to impoverishment standards by paying for the necessary care. Assets that have taken a lifetime to accumulate can be wiped out in a few months.

Whether or not it is ethical to divest yourself of assets to qualify for government programs is not the purpose of this chapter. Some will argue that taxpayers are hurt when someone gives away money or property to qualify for government benefits. But only certain government benefit programs have an asset test to qualify. Medicare is funded through premiums paid over the life of the beneficiaries. However, much of Medicare costs today are actually paid by taxpayer dollars, because the system costs more than it takes in. Why doesn't the government have an asset test for people who place an undue burden on Medicare? What about tax planning? Is it ethical for many to use legal strategies to avoid paying taxes? As an illustration of how this all works, consider this example:

Two 85-year-old friends, Bill and Ed, have to stay in a nursing home to receive the care they need. They both worked all their lives and retired with enough income from pensions and Social Security to live comfortably. Both had houses with no mortgages or liens. Bill saved all his life and never spent money on vacations or things for himself. He had accumulated $300,000 in an investment account. On the other hand, Ed had enjoyed all the good things in life for himself and his family and now had about $12,000 in a savings account.

The cost of their care is the same, about $10,000 each month. Ed will be considered eligible for Medicaid to immediately pay for his care. Bill will have to spend about $275,000 on his care before Medicaid will consider him "impoverished" and then pay for his care. Is it wrong for Bill to want to receive the same benefit from the government as his friend? Was he foolish to have saved his money and now want to leave some for his children?

Why People Plan

Some couples plan ahead so they can be sure to have enough assets and income for the surviving spouse to live on. Social Security will be reduced to one payment instead of two after the death of the first spouse. Many times the retirement pension of the first spouse is reduced or eliminated at his or her death. I know husbands who will refuse care because they are worried about the costs and what it will do to the lifestyle of the wife they leave behind.

Other people have planned and saved all their lives to pay off their mortgage so they can leave the house to their children. For some reason, this asset means more to people with meager savings because they have worked so hard to finally "own it." It has been their intention that at least their kids will get the house. Others who have saved more money may also want to leave some of it for their children. They will not ask for the help they need because this gift is so important to them. Fear of leaving nothing behind is real and should be taken into consideration when people are faced with long-term care choices.

I can tell you that my parents never had a lot of money they planned to leave as an inheritance. They had both worked, provided us with a wonderful home, and we were happy. All of us had successfully moved on to our own lives and were not planning on receiving money when they died. But for my parents themselves, the amount of money required to pay for care was a shock. Mom and Dad had never stayed in a hotel that had cost even $150 per night. Now, the nursing home wanted $300 for every day my father was required to stay beyond the days that Medicare would cover.

My father was worried about how my mom would get by if they had to spend all their savings on his care. They were of a generation that had been taught to save for a rainy day and to be able to pay for the things they needed. They had paid off their credit-card bill each month. Like many people, they never lived beyond their means and saved as much as they could. Mom cut coupons and they bought savings bonds to put money aside for security.

My parents' sense of security was threatened by the overwhelming cost of long-term care. Dad's pension would be cut in half when he died, and Mom would be living on one Social Security check. For people who never thought of asking anyone else for help, the prospect of impoverishment was all of a sudden a reality. Financial insecurity is a very real part of getting older and becomes another worry along with the physical decline elders are already experiencing. To relieve these burdens, it is really important that families receive proper advice at this time.

Planning Techniques to Use in Advance

Irrevocable income-only trust: One of the most successful planning techniques is to place assets into an irrevocable trust so as to remove them from the ownership of the older person or couple. As a basic concept, the senior doing estate planning places assets into a trust that can allow him or her to receive the income generated by these assets, while not having direct access to the principal. Because you have given up access and control of the assets in the trust, those assets will not be considered available for Medicaid purposes.

The transfer of assets into the trust will cause a penalty until the current look-back period of 60 months has expired. When properly drafted, the trust can provide both asset protection and tax benefits (elimination of capital gains and gift taxes, as well as retention of real property tax exemptions) and avoid the probate process for the assets that are held in the trust.

Typically, the terms of the trust provide that all of the income (interest, dividends, etc.) can be paid to the person or persons who establish the trust and whose money is used to fund the trust. The trustee simply pays the income produced by the assets in the trust to the grantor or grantors.

The terms of the trust should further provide that none of the principal of the trust (which would be distributions above and beyond income) would be payable to the grantor or grantors. Otherwise, if principal could be payable, the trust would be considered an available resource by the Department of Social Services (the local agency administering the Medicaid program) and have to be used to pay for long-term care costs. That being said, the trust can provide for principal distributions to be made to the grantor's children (or other named beneficiaries of the trust), who could then informally gift monies back to the grantor, if they so desired.

After five years from the date on which the last of your assets are transferred to the trust, the entire principal of the trust is protected from the costs of skilled nursing. However, since you and/or your spouse would always be entitled to the income on the trust, this income is always considered available to pay for your long-term care costs.

The month following the month in which all of the assets are placed into the trust, you and/or your spouse could apply for one of the *Community Medicaid Waiver* programs, which could provide care to you and/or your spouse at home, without any sanction, because there is currently no look-back period for Community Medicaid programs.

Income on the trust will be taxed to you and your spouse as the grantors, since this is a "grantor trust" for income tax purposes. It is important to note that the trustees will have to file a separate income tax return each year for the trust, because the trust will have a separate tax ID number. However, instead of the trust paying the tax, the trustees will give you and/or your spouse a statement that itemizes the income you need to claim on your personal income tax returns along with your other income. Therefore, your income tax liability should be the same as it always was, even if you have this type of trust.

Your children, or whomever you name as beneficiaries of the trust, will receive a stepped-up cost basis for all of your stocks and other assets in the trust, except for annuities. This means that when they sell the stocks or real property after your deaths, they will pay capital gains tax only on the difference between the value at your death and the value on the date that the assets are sold, instead of the difference between what you originally paid for the asset and the value at the time they sell it.

The trust will also avoid probate for the assets that are owned by it. In other words, your last will and testament will not have to be probated in the surrogate court when you die in order to distribute these assets to your beneficiaries. As a result, your children and other beneficiaries will not have to pay any court filing fees or legal fees associated with administering an estate. Unlike probate, there will be no time delays in distributing the assets in your trust. By law, an estate in probate must remain open for seven months from the date an executor is appointed before it can be closed.

The grantors can have the right to change the ultimate beneficiaries of the trust by using a limited power of appointment, which can be retained in the trust document. Therefore, you or your spouse can change whom you want to receive the money in the trust as many times as you like before you die. Grantors can also retain the right to remove one or more of the trustees, for any reason. If you don't like something that the trustees are doing, you can appoint anyone else (except yourselves) as the trustee.

A trust can protect your money from the claims of your children's creditors. Until you both pass away and the money is distributed to the beneficiaries, their creditors cannot get at it. Furthermore, the monies in the trust are protected from your children's spouses in a divorce proceeding.

If the trust owns your primary residence, you can be given the exclusive right to occupy and enjoy the property and this should also preserve all of the real estate exemptions (like school tax or veterans) that you had before you transferred it into the

A simple deed transfer to your children can protect your property while allowing you access to Medicaid benefits.

trust. In addition, your trustee can sell the residence and use the proceeds to purchase a different home.

If you or your spouse should need skilled-nursing home care before the expiration of the 60-month look-back period, the trust can be revoked. Revocation of an irrevocable trust can be done, but all interested parties must consent to any amendment or revocation. In this situation, an outright gift and promissory note plan may be appropriate to preserve assets from long-term care costs (see below).

Life-estate deed transfer: Many people want to know how to protect their home, even if everything else they have saved may have to be spent on care. If this is the only asset you are seeking to protect, a simple deed transfer to your children with a retained life estate for yourself can protect the property and still allow you to access Medicaid benefits as well as preserve your current real estate tax exemptions.

What is a *life estate?* Simply, it is an ownership of real property that will last for the term of a person's life. The people who will take the property upon the death of the life tenant are called *remaindermen.* Think of it as a way to divide the ownership of real property over time. The remaindermen are given a *future interest* in the property, but the deed is filed now to remove that portion from your ownership so you no longer own the whole thing.

Make sure that your deed retains a life estate for you. There are several reasons you do not want to make an outright gift of your home to your children. If you sell your home, the sale is currently exempt from state and federal income tax, up to a profit of $250,000 for each spouse. If your children sell the property after it has been gifted to them during your life, they may have to pay capital gains tax because it is not their primary residence. By giving them the property outright during your lifetime, they receive it with a cost basis of what you paid for the property plus capital improvements.

Although the remaindermen do not have a current right to occupy the premises, they are given an ownership interest in the property at the time the deed is filed. This is how it becomes a tool for Medicaid planning. Because someone else is given part ownership of the house now, you no longer own the "entire" asset. During the lifetimes of the life estate owners, the residence is currently not considered an asset for Medicaid eligibility. Because you have transferred an interest in property, the transaction will be subject to a penalty during the duration of the look-back period for Medicaid.

If you want to sell your house during your lifetime, the people to whom you have given the remainder interest must also agree to the sale. However, you can and should retain a power of appointment in the deed language. This will allow you to change the people to whom the remainder is given. By using this power, you can change the ownership to a child who will agree to the sale if there is a problem with consent from one of the parties. In addition, by keeping this power to change the terms of the deed, the transfer to your children is considered incomplete for gift tax purposes. This means that you do not have to file a gift tax return when you file the deed granting the property.

As mentioned in an earlier chapter, if you think the property may likely be sold before your death, then it may be a better idea to protect the property using an irrevocable trust. If the property is sold during your lifetime using the life-estate deed, you will be entitled to a portion of the sale proceeds. The amount will be calculated based on your life expectancy at the time of the sale. Your children will also not receive the stepped-up basis that they would have if they waited to sell until after your death.

Purchasing a life estate in another property: When planning for parents who may no longer want or be able to safely live on their own, some children would like to have them move into their home. This way the family members can be close by and even provide assistance with their daily needs. Family caregiving is usually done out of love and a true desire to be closer to each other. However, this living arrangement can also provide an opportunity for the elderly person to reduce the assets that might otherwise have to be spent paying for care in the future. Mom or Dad can purchase a life estate in the child's home where they will be living. Put simply, this is the purchase of a legal right to live in the home for the rest of their life. After the person entitled to the life estate passes away, full legal ownership of the property will once again be held by the child.

As far as Medicaid is concerned, the assets used to purchase the life estate will not be considered an uncompensated transfer (i.e., a transfer for less than fair-market value), as long as the life estate is purchased for fair-market value and the purchaser resides in the home for at least one year after the purchase. This technique is used to reduce the assets owned by a senior that might otherwise have to be spent on nursing home services in the future.

Personal service contracts: As we all know, most long-term care is provided by family members or friends and is done out of love and affection. Generally, there are no financial arrangements made and the services are provided for free. However, if these services are provided according to the terms of a properly drafted contract called a *caregiver agreement,* family members can get paid for the care they provide and legally reduce the assets of the person receiving care. These caregiver agreements must follow strict rules to be considered valid. Otherwise Medicaid will consider the payments as gifts.

For Medicaid eligibility purposes, fair-market value must be received for the assets transferred under the contract. Consequently, the contract cannot stipulate that services will be given "as needed" because it cannot be determined that fair-market value will be received in this way. For Medicaid to confirm what services were provided, fair-market compensation must be charged and stated under the contract and credible documentation must be kept. Pay rates are expected to comply with the handbook developed by the U.S. Department of Labor.

If the contract provides for a lump-sum payment, the contract must require the return of any prepaid money if the care recipient dies before his or her calculated life expectancy. In addition, services cannot be provided while someone is in a nursing home receiving care. Furthermore, you cannot create a caregiver agreement for services already provided. Caregivers are required to pay all federal, state, and employment taxes on the income they earn. As you can see, this type of arrangement is not easily established and should be done with the advice of an experienced elder law attorney.

Something else to consider: other children may have conflicting opinions about this type of arrangement. It may be a good idea to have all family members agree even if they will not be providing care.

Planning Techniques to Use in a Crisis

Spend down to Medicaid levels: As discussed earlier, a penalty will be assessed for giving assets away. However, there is no limit on how a Medicaid applicant or her spouse may spend their money. There is still time to protect assets by spending on things that you need or want. Some things that people consider:

• *Making repairs to the home:* get the new roof that you need; improve the bathroom so that it is more accessible for the older spouse still living at home; improve the driveway.

• *Updating home furnishings:* replace the old throw rugs with carpeting; update the kitchen; do the things you would never do for yourself because you were saving your money for old age!

• *Getting a new car*: you may now be driving to and from the nursing home every day and an updated car will be safer and require less maintenance.

• *Finding a new residence*: if the home is two stories and the community spouse will still be walking upstairs for the bathroom and down to the basement to do the laundry, why not consider moving to a patio home or ranch house that will be more accommodating for an older lifestyle? Because the home-equity exemption amount may be very high, a lot of money can be exempted from Medicaid consideration by spending it on a new primary residence. This could be something to greatly improve the life of the community spouse who is currently going through so much stress and worry.

Prepaying burial accounts: One of the simplest ways to reduce excess resources is to prepay irrevocable funeral arrangements. With the cost of a traditional funeral approaching $15,000 in some places, this can be a way to pay now for an expense that will otherwise have to be paid in the future anyway. You can make these arrangements for the applicant and his or her spouse; children and their spouses; and the applicant's parents, brothers and sisters, and their spouses.

These prepaid irrevocable burial accounts are usually purchased through a funeral home under the terms of a contract. The contract will itemize the merchandise and services purchased and will justify the total price paid by the applicant. The contact can include burial space items and related services except for food, lodging, and transportation expenses for family or guests.

Gift and promissory note strategy: *Caution: this is a bit complicated!* If you have significant excess resources that cannot be spent down quickly, or transfers that have occurred within the look-back period that cannot be returned and will cause a penalty upon Medicaid application, this may be a strategy to consider. For this strategy to work, careful attention must be paid to the legal details, and I would not advise it without the help of competent counsel.

A gift and note strategy entails the use of two transfers. The amount of the two transfers together will equal the amount of excess resources.

Transfer 1: The first transfer will be the amount of money that can be preserved by making a gift. The amount can also include uncompensated transfers made during the past five years that will not be paid back. By making this gift, we can be sure that a penalty will be assessed when applying for Medicaid.

Transfer 2: The second transfer will be made in exchange for a promissory note that meets all the compliance requirements for Medicaid under the Deficit Reduction Act rules. Medicaid rules require that the note be irrevocable, actuarially sound, non-negotiable, and not prepaid. The terms of the promissory note set up a schedule that will pay out during the period of ineligibility that will be assessed by Medicaid. The note is calculated so that the monthly payments, when combined with the applicant's other income, equal an amount slightly less than the actual cost of the nursing-home care during the month that coverage is first requested.

Medicaid will determine the number of months to which a penalty will be applied. The applicant will be entitled to limited coverage by Medicaid, which means that Medicaid will pay for some medical expenses but not for skilled-nursing services during that period of time. Then, each month during that period, the monthly note payment is made from the holder of the note directly into the bank account of the applicant. The applicant then uses the deposited funds to pay the nursing-home bill for that month. Records of these transactions must be kept meticulously. At the end of the penalty period and the end of the note, the applicant will be eligible for Medicaid.

The result of the gift and note strategy will be that excess resources are eliminated and eligibility is accelerated by half the time that it would have normally taken. Most important, you have preserved a portion of the excess resources that would otherwise have had to be spent on care.

Home-care option: Under current Medicaid rules, community-based assistance programs do not require the 60-month look-back associated with nursing-home Medicaid. Therefore, as of 2014, there will be no gifting penalties for transferring assets to reach the required asset levels. However, if either spouse requires nursing care in a facility within the original 60-month look-back period, gifting penalties will be assessed at that time. As we have discussed, the care needs of older people are constantly changing.

While home care may be appropriate at the beginning, the person's medical condition may deteriorate over time and nurs-

Medicaid and the 'Gift and Note' Strategy

If you are currently paying for skilled nursing services and have "excess resources," they will have to be "spent down" before you can apply for Medicaid.

By using two transfers described below—one a gift, the other a promissory note—you could help preserve some of those resources and accelerate your eligibility for Medicaid. Here is a simplified example:*

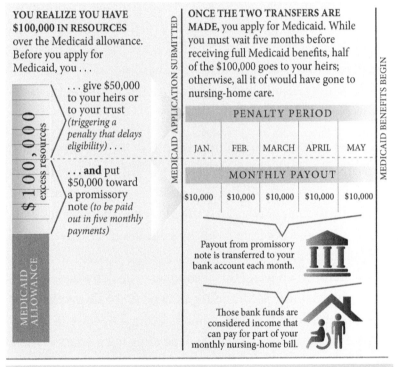

YOU REALIZE YOU HAVE $100,000 IN RESOURCES over the Medicaid allowance. Before you apply for Medicaid, you . . .

. . . give $50,000 to your heirs or to your trust *(triggering a penalty that delays eligibility)* . . .

. . . **and** put $50,000 toward a promissory note *(to be paid out in five monthly payments)*

$100,000 excess resources

MEDICAID ALLOWANCE

MEDICAID APPLICATION SUBMITTED

ONCE THE TWO TRANSFERS ARE MADE, you apply for Medicaid. While you must wait five months before receiving full Medicaid benefits, half of the $100,000 goes to your heirs; otherwise, all it of would have gone to nursing-home care.

MEDICAID BENEFITS BEGIN

PENALTY PERIOD

| JAN. | FEB. | MARCH | APRIL | MAY |

MONTHLY PAYOUT

| $10,000 | $10,000 | $10,000 | $10,000 | $10,000 |

Payout from promissory note is transferred to your bank account each month.

Those bank funds are considered income that can pay for part of your monthly nursing-home bill.

WITH PLAN:
$50,000 *to heirs /* **$50,000** *to nursing home /* **5 months** *until Medicaid eligibility*

WITHOUT PLAN:
None *to heirs /* **$100,000** *to nursing home /* **10 months** *until Medicaid eligibility*

*Numbers are approximate for calculations that are more complex and specific than those shown in the example.

ing-home placement could become necessary within 60 months. This is another reason for the family to have competent and caring counsel who will stay involved as the plan progresses.

By starting with home care at the beginning, there may still be time to implement a gifting plan for individuals who may need minimal help now. The family can apply for home-care benefits and get the clock started for the 60-month look-back. This could potentially save a significant amount of nursing-home payments in the future. Let me reiterate: if an individual can live at home with the assistance of home care, it is possible to transfer assets and qualify for Medicaid immediately to cover those costs.

Treatment of IRAs in crisis planning: If an IRA or other qualified retirement account is paying out periodic payments that are actuarially sound for Medicaid purposes, then the principal of that asset will not count as an available resource to pay for care. Only the income generated will be considered in determining Medicaid eligibility.

Be careful when using this technique—the definition of periodic payments under Medicaid regulations is not always the same as required minimum distributions as defined by the IRS. A distinction is made in the calculation depending upon whether there is a community spouse. If there is one, the principal of the retirement account will be exempt if distributions are made pursuant to IRS requirements. If there is no community spouse, the applicant must maximize her periodic payments according to life expectancy tables set forth by the Department of Social Services.

Sometimes it may be better (or necessary) to liquidate the money in a retirement account, rather than have it considered as income only. The determination should be made based on considerations like:

- what is the life expectancy of the applicant, and what are her other resources?
- how much will the periodic payment be that will have to be spent on care?
- what are the income tax consequences of the liquidation?

If someone will be privately paying for care, using retirement income to pay for that may be beneficial because the income tax accrued may be deductible as a medical expense at the same time. All of these considerations should be discussed with your accountant and financial adviser, in conjunction with counsel who understands the Medicaid consequences.

The next chapter will expand on the reasons for having multiple advisers to ensure that your planning is comprehensive and that your decisions all fit together for your benefit.

8

IT TAKES A TEAM

OULD YOU READ A BOOK or go to a seminar about heart surgery and then try to do it yourself? Better yet, would you have your podiatrist perform the heart operation? (After all, they are both doctors!)

You need a plan that will help you sleep at night, not give you new things to worry about. We will discuss some planning examples in the next chapter.

I give seminars all the time and some people come more than once. But often they don't follow through—they don't actually create documents or move their money. Many think that all lawyers are the same, and they go back to their family friend who is a real estate attorney and hire her to plan their estate. I frequently see their families at my office when a crisis arises.

Hopefully this book has given you some of the information you will need as you begin to plan for, receive, and pay for the care you may need later in life. However, when the time comes, you will be required to make important decisions and take definitive action. You will quickly realize that you want an adviser experienced in this field to help you.

Knowledge is very helpful, but it cannot take the place of professional help when confronted with the need for long-term care. Navigating the disorganized array of programs, services, payment sources, and regulations that abound in the system requires professional experience. Trying to do it alone will only increase your stress, cost you more in the long run, and could even end up being a source of family conflict.

As I mentioned in the preface to this book, families have difficulty navigating the complex and confusing array of long-term support and services because they are administered by multiple private and public agencies with complex and sometimes conflicting rules and regulations. Services are provided in a fragmented, uncoordinated system by disparate agencies, each with their own funding, rules, and processes.

I have spent my career trying to help clients navigate this "system." It is only through commitment, trial and error, and serendipitous findings of otherwise obscure programs or services that my ability to help people has improved. It has very little to do with changes or improvements to what currently exists—an unwieldy, complicated, and disconnected mess of a long-term care system.

So what does a smart person who really wants the best care and support for a loved one do? In my opinion, the process takes a team of knowledgeable professionals from several areas who will work together and with you, to create a plan that will work.

To be successful, your plan will need to coordinate information in three key areas:

- financial
- legal
- health care.

In our local area (Western New York), there is a network of professionals who work in the field of long-term care who meet regularly to help coordinate services for clients. We conduct educational meetings to learn about new programs and regulations that affect the elderly population. Members of an organization like this are able to recommend the right contacts for you to get the services you need. By understanding, in advance, the options for care settings and which ones may be appropriate, the process will be better for everyone involved. Prior knowledge will save money and time, and will prevent crisis planning.

Making use of professional advisers at this point will be the most efficient and effective use of your time. A professional geriatric-care manager will be an invaluable resource and should be part of your team. An elder law attorney can help you understand which government programs may be available to pay for the services you need. The expertise that can be provided by a

A professional geriatric-care manager will be an invaluable resource and should be part of your team.

long-term care professional will likely save you many times the money you spend for the advice.

All of this is hard. Nothing is the way it was and everyone would like to have his or her "old life" back. But we are in new territory called long-term care and, subsequently, this is a new stage of life. Try to look at it as a new chapter—find joys at each step. Remember, no one wants to need help, but we all may face this situation if we live long enough. I remember my mom saying to me that she couldn't wait for my dad to get back to driving again so it could be like it was just a few months ago. That is when I realized that it was never going to be "the way it was" again for them. Dad wasn't going to get younger and I couldn't move back the clock. We had to love each other through the process of aging and decline. I am so happy I was able to help them get through it with the least amount of stress and the greatest amount of love.

Professional Services

Some of the professions that have evolved to provide services for people needing long-term care include:

- geriatric-care managers
- elder law and estate planning attorneys
- Certified Financial Planners
- professional home-care services
- home maintenance and modification
- senior relocation and real estate professionals
- preplanning funeral providers
- elder-mediation services

- geriatric physician services
- home-alert and monitoring systems
- bill-paying assistance
- adult day-care providers
- formal care settings (such as assisted-living and skilled-nursing facilities)
- dementia-care facilities
- hospice care
- long-term care insurance specialists.

These professionals spend their full time addressing one area of need you may encounter. However, your overall success will depend upon the coordinated efforts of many of them. I try to create "teams" of professionals who will work together for the benefit of my clients. It works best if you can get the family and professionals to meet so that everyone is on the same page.

Given the current system, it takes someone committed to the big picture to compel all of the separate working parts to come together. By sheer force of will, I have been able to do this, but I must admit that most of my colleagues still work in silos. Most families still end up having to fit the pieces together by themselves.

Geriatric-care management: I have found it invaluable to work directly with a geriatric-care manager to create and implement plans for my elderly clients. As professionals, care managers usually have a background in nursing or social work. They are trained to evaluate the abilities and needs of the elderly and to recommend and establish appropriate care.

For example, sometimes I visit the homes of my clients so they can sign a document there. It is often obvious they are not doing well and need assistance. Though I work with these issues every day, I am not qualified to assess their level of need, nor can I suggest a specific care plan. When a geriatric-care manager meets with my clients and their families, she can help by doing things like:

- assess the level and type of care needed
- develop a plan of care
- include the family in the planning process
- make sure the care will be given in a safe and appropriate place
- reduce family stress by getting everyone on the same page
- coordinate the duties of family members and other supports
- get the care plan started by arranging with home-care agencies selected by the family
- arrange for day care to relieve the primary caregiver at least part time
- work with elder law attorneys to help clients qualify for government programs that may pay for the required services.

After the plan is started, changes will inevitably take place. By conducting ongoing assessments, a care manager can implement changes to the plan and continue to support the family along the way. Sometimes a move to assisted living or nursing-home care becomes appropriate. The care manager can then act as an advocate for the family during the admissions process.

I have worked with a care manager to get families out of situations that have become unworkable. For example, Mom says she can't afford to pay for a caregiver and all of the kids have full-time jobs. They take turns being with Mom at night and in the morning, but she is left alone all day. After her second hospitalization for falling while alone, the family seeks help at my office.

By bringing in a care manager, we were able to arrange for Mom to be picked up and taken to a local day-care program. Now she enjoys the company of new friends and we have solved the problem of her being alone all day. The family understands that this arrangement will work for a time, but when Mom begins to need additional assistance, they have a team of professionals who will help adjust the plan accordingly. Hiring a care manager can be an especially good decision for family members who live far away. These managers can be a local contact to monitor the safety and health of your mom or dad.

The results of a *comprehensive geriatric-care assessment* help determine possible issues and suggest how needs can best be met. Functional ability is measured on the basis of:

- *basic activities of daily living (ADLs):* daily self-care activities like eating, dressing, bathing, using the toilet, transferring into and out of a chair

- *instrumental activities of daily living:* activities that allow a person to live independently in his home, such as shopping, cooking, managing finances, using the telephone, and taking medication properly

- *advanced ADLs:* independent activities like driving, gardening, and traveling

- *physical status:* review of medical history, physical examination, vision test, hearing test, gait and balance tests

- *cognitive and mental health:* cognitive ability and memory issues, anxiety or depression

- *social assessment:* social interaction, friends, and determination of current and potential caregivers

- *environmental assessment:* physical environment safety, physical barriers like stairs, bathroom access, transportation to doctors, etc.

- *nutrition, sleep, and medications:* review and assess.

There is a lot to consider and professionals can help determine whether the required level of care can continue to be met in the home, or if a more formal setting would be appropriate. This determination will involve medical, social, and financial input. Figuring how to pay for the services will be key. Many resources are available to seniors that most families don't know about. You should meet with a knowledgeable elder law attorney for this information.

Elder Law and Estate Planning Attorney

Throughout this book you have learned about the many issues that are part of my daily work as an elder law attorney. If the attorney is involved and caring, a wide range of concerns can be addressed with his or her help. Here is a partial list of services that can be provided by an elder law and estate planning attorney:

- legal advice for transferring your assets and real property to your heirs in the most efficient manner

- drafting appropriate legal documents, including wills, trusts, and deeds
- completing advance directives like powers of attorney and health-care proxies
- planning with your accountant to avoid estate and capital gains taxes and to minimize income taxes
- planning to prevent impoverishment of a spouse when the other spouse requires care
- planning strategies to accelerate Medicaid approval, qualification, and application assistance
- planning for incapacity and care management
- financial-management coordination with your adviser to implement planning and distribution of assets
- help with the delegation of decision making for financial and health-care issues and working with your family to implement plans
- assistance with management of trusts and estates
- performing probate services
- coordinated work with geriatric-management professionals for placements in assisted-living and skilled-nursing facilities.

Financial Planning

The process of determining what assets you own and how they are titled can be time-consuming and may seem overwhelming at first. We spend our lifetime accumulating assets of various kinds and at different times. For example, many of my clients have purchased life insurance policies to cover the cost of burial needs. Most of these policies have not been reviewed in years and may contain almost as much cash value as they will pay at death. Retirement accounts from different employers may have been rolled into various IRAs. Recently, banks have been selling annuities to clients in place of other traditional savings vehicles because they offer higher interest rates.

It can be an interesting endeavor to uncover the variety of places individuals and couples have stashed their money. We have to discover all of it, because it is very important to know everything people own as we begin to plan for long-term care.

Most people come into older age with a mix of investments accumulated over the years. Many older people do not have a clear picture of their financial situation and have not shared all of this information with their family. However, as I have said, this information is critically important before any planning or advice can be provided. Many people have done some planning of their own, like adding others as joint owners on their bank accounts or CDs. People can now specify that certain assets "transfer on death" directly to their heirs. Failure to uncover the true nature of each asset can result in conflicting instructions and unintended consequences.

Some people make frequent changes to their financial accounts and may have a trusted adviser who has helped them. Others have simply accumulated a variety of investments over

It can be an interesting endeavor to uncover the variety of places individuals and couples have stashed their money.

their lifetime and do not have a coordinated picture. In either case, it is important to have informed financial advice when considering changes to their portfolios.

I have had some clients who have never trusted anyone else to invest their wealth, and they are very protective of this control. I work hard to help them understand that even the smartest investor will someday have to hand over the job. If a wife is left without proper guidance after years in the dark, it can be a source of additional strain after the death of her husband. Finding someone you trust with this information is critical. A lawyer can help with some advice in this regard, but a competent and trustworthy family member or financial adviser will be necessary at some point. Why not select, while you are alive, someone you can trust who will be able to help the family manage what you have accumulated after you are gone?

To prepare a financial plan for long-term care, we have to know everything about a person's assets, including life insurance, bank accounts, retirement and investment accounts, annuities, bonds, and any other resources. Some financial advisers have taken an extra step in their education and obtained the designation as a Certified Financial Planner. These individuals have a broad knowledge base and should be able to help when organizing a wide variety of investments. I encourage my clients to consider using such a professional when we get together and transfer assets as part of the plan.

I encourage all of my older clients to consolidate their financial life. In most cases, someone else can manage the assets without changing the composition of a diversified portfolio. Most investment companies can hold a variety of investments and report them on one statement. This makes life a lot easier for your power of attorney to step in, if necessary. It is a good idea to bring the people you expect to manage your assets in the future to your planning meetings.

The best plans include family members so that everyone is on the same page as to how money will be handled. Even if you have given formal authority to one of your children, invite everyone who wants to be included. This way there will be less suspicion or questioning among siblings when someone has to take action. Select a financial adviser who will take the time to meet with your family and your lawyer so that everyone understands the plan.

There are many types of financial professionals. Some people have used a friend or relative in the industry to help them with investment purchases. Often these advisers are insurance agents who have sold them a variety of life insurance policies and annuities. Other people use advisers at their local bank branch for investment services or to buy annuity products. Many times, these investments are insurance products not owned or managed by the bank. I have found that many seniors do not understand the complicated rules that accompany such products and that surrender charges may be imposed if these assets have to be used or moved.

A financial adviser who regularly works with the elderly will understand how to manage assets that may be needed to pay for care. They will work closely with your elder law attorney to make sure that your asset structure is prepared for disability, incapacity, or death. It is important to have a financial adviser on your team to provide services such as:

- investment advice appropriate for current and future income needs
- insurance planning
- asset allocation
- income tax planning.

Just like any other relationship with a professional adviser, your investment counselor should be someone you trust. You should be able to tell her about your whole investment picture. You can't get good advice from a doctor if she doesn't know about all your problems. The same is true for your investments. At this important time of your financial life, it is imperative to work with someone experienced in comprehensive planning. I like to work with advisers who have achieved the Certified Financial Planner (CFP) designation.

Elder Mediation

In my opinion, mediation should be recommended as a first course of action when families with eldercare issues have come to such an impasse that they seek legal help to resolve them. Unfortunately, disputes over caregiving or the division of family property routinely end up being settled in a courtroom. I believe lawyers should be willing to offer mediation as an alternative to litigation. The surrogate court is an expensive and very public place to hash out old sibling rivalries. Mediation offers a better chance for family relationships to survive the process. In many cases, family members can come to an agreement they can live with, rather than having a judge decide a winner and a loser.

Litigation and courtrooms are intimidating even to the young and healthy. Elderly family members should be offered every alternative to this experience. Resolving family disputes through court proceedings is expensive and uses up the money that Mom and Dad hoped would be given to their children. One outcome of mediation may be a commitment to respect and value each party's opinion; family members also are often given tools to communicate more effectively in the future. Mediation is also private. Parties can keep the details of their family disputes out of the public eye. My mother would always remind me, "What will the neighbors think?" I can't imagine the internal horror felt by many an elderly parent seeing her family's dirty laundry paraded through court.

Mediation of eldercare disputes is in its infancy and I am one of the proponents of its use. As I write this, I co-chair a committee of the New York State Bar Association working to expand the practice.

Putting It All Together

Planning for eldercare requires a team approach. The most cost-effective and efficient way to navigate the fragmented providers and confusing array of services is by using a coordinated team of professionals. The experience that comes from dealing with countless similar challenges, along with the education and training of professionals, makes their help invaluable.

Professional advisers working in this field don't always communicate effectively with one another. There has to be at least one adviser who takes the lead—bringing the legal, financial, and caregiving requirements into focus. The family should be involved in any planning meetings. If key members of the family support group are out of town, they can be conferenced-in to key conversations. Important documents should be in the hands of those who will need to use them as issues arise.

9

Planning Is the Key

THE FOLLOWING EXAMPLES ILLUSTRATE how professional assistance can recommend options you may not have otherwise considered (names have been changed to protect privacy).

Ed Schultz

My client Ed Schultz is an 85-year-old World War II veteran. He never married, lives alone, and can no longer drive. He spends most of his time alone and isn't eating as much or as well as he should. He goes to the VA for his medical treatment. He asked at the VA for possible assistance at home, but they told him he has "too much money."

After meeting Mr. Schultz, I find that he gets Meals on Wheels, which he doesn't really like. However, he does enjoy going to his niece's house for dinner. I review his documents and realize that his power of attorney doesn't allow for transfers of assets. Should he become unable to manage his own finances, we could do no other planning without a guardianship proceeding, unless he could still sign a new power of attorney that included the necessary provision. He has Social Security and pension income of $2,300 per month. His savings total $120,000 and he has an IRA of $20,000.

Mr. Schultz and I meet with a geriatric-care manager who visits his home and makes a personal and safety assessment. His refrigerator contents indicate a lack of interest in food and he is afraid of taking a shower because he might fall. In his case, we suggested two good options:

• He might move to a local assisted-living facility that could provide better meals and help him bathe. He would also enjoy the company of other people every day. The cost would be around $4,000 each month. He doesn't think he can afford it. We can explain that his money is there for him to use to supplement his income. He has never spent his savings on himself before! But when I tell him that the VA could supplement his income to meet the cost, his ears perk up.

We could move his resources that are above VA requirements (according to VA current standards, somewhere below $80,000) into a trust. Then the VA Aid and Attendance pension of $1,758 could be added to his monthly income, and he could see a way to afford the facility. He wouldn't have to worry about running out of money. Should he need to move to a skilled-nursing facility, his assets would have to be spent down to $14,500. If he made it through five years at assisted living, the penalty for the transfer for VA purposes would no longer be a problem. Otherwise, we could revoke the trust and do other planning at that time.

• If Mr. Schultz really wanted to remain in his home, we could do the same plan and apply for Aid and Attendance benefits to help pay for home care at first. If he needed more services, we could transfer additional money to the trust and apply for Community Medicaid to cover his home care. He could go to a VA day care during the day for socialization, and Medicaid could provide transportation.

We would encourage his niece to help him prepay for his funeral. I would redo his power of attorney and discuss his intentions for the distribution of his estate at death. If he wants to avoid more legal costs and probate, I would tell him that his trust already does that! I would then work with him to make sure that any accounts held outside of the trust would also avoid probate when he passes away. We would update his IRA beneficiaries and complete transfer-on-death forms at the bank.

Tom and Dorothy Mitchell

This couple first came to me two years ago and we completed some basic planning for them at that time. Tom had already suffered several strokes, but was still functioning well on his own. They signed powers of attorney and we reviewed their finances. The Mitchells had recently moved into a new patio home with an aging-friendly floor plan. We completed a property transfer of the remainder interest in the patio home to their two children, to avoid probate and protect the value of the property, should they both require nursing care. Their asset combination was unusual in that almost all of their savings were held in Tom's very large retirement account (IRA), with only a small amount of "after-tax" money in the bank. They had a very comfortable monthly income that they used for day-to-day living. Tom's annual required minimum distribution from his IRA was put in the bank or used to help their children.

Tom is now 75 and has suffered a severe stroke that left him unable to swallow and in need of constant supervision. Dorothy brought him home from the hospital and has learned to use a suction machine and how to feed him through his tube. As a result of his hospitalization, Tom is receiving about six hours of home care per week and physical and speech/swallow therapy, paid for by Medicare. Dorothy is 68 and is left to do the rest of the caregiving on her own. She has hired private aides to help her during the night and for a few hours each day, paying them collectively about $2,500 every week.

Because we had reviewed the Mitchells' assets with their financial consultant during our initial planning, they knew to call us when Dorothy asked about taking money from Tom's IRA to pay the $10,000 monthly bill. First I met with Dorothy alone at my office to find out how she was doing. She was trying hard to be optimistic but was getting tired from being in charge of her husband's care 24 hours a day. At least she was getting sleep at night now, and she had seen some progress in his condition. I visited their home with a geriatric-care manager to determine if Tom might be a good fit for a home-care program provided by Medicaid, called Nursing

Home Transition and Diversion. This was the program we used for my father, which allowed him to remain in his home while receiving 24-hour aide service.

Tom is eligible for this Medicaid program because their countable assets are already below Medicaid eligibility levels. His large IRA is not counted as an asset, but his required minimum distribution will have to be used to help pay for the care. It could take some time before the wheels of bureaucracy turn and he is approved for both Medicaid and the diversion program, but after that, they would not have to pay privately for his care. I don't think Dorothy can continue for an extended period of time without additional help, and Tom's needs may increase. She is still young and will need the IRA to live on after Tom is gone. If she wants Tom to remain at home, this program could provide a solution.

The aides currently providing Tom's care are not licensed or monitored by anyone but Dorothy. As their employer, she is technically responsible for their taxes. If anything happens to them on the job, she could be held liable. These are additional worries that will be relieved by using the services of an agency approved and monitored by the Medicaid program. Government-approved companies must meet legal and operating standards set by each state's department of health.

After Tom has been approved for the diversion program, he will be given a case supervisor, who will make sure he has the appropriate number of hours, given his home situation. The hours can increase if his condition declines. Dorothy will have to update her will and beneficiary designations to leave only the required amount to Tom, should she pass away before him.

David and Sandy Butler

David came in to see me with his adult son, Michael, who was visiting from out of town. David's wife, Sandy, has had Alzheimer's disease for about seven years. Both of their children live in other states. David had kept Sandy home and cared for her by himself for as long as he could. For the past three years she has been living in the dementia unit of an assisted-living facility. He just received notice last week that she can no longer be cared for at this level and that she will have to move to the skilled facility in their town.

The Butlers' assets include their home and a large retirement account from David's work at the university. To pay for her care at assisted living, David has been withdrawing $5,000 each month from his retirement account. He maintains his lifestyle on their remaining Social Security income. Before coming to see me, he had called the administrator of his retirement plan and increased the distributions to $10,000 per month, to be able to pay for her care at the nursing home.

After reviewing to make sure that I knew the extent of any other assets, I was able to give David some welcome good news! I told him that he could call the retirement plan back and tell them that he required only his minimum distribution amount each month. The assets in his retirement account are not counted toward Medicaid eligibility. As a result, Sandy was eligible for Medicaid to pay the bill at the nursing home.

10

MAYBE WE CAN LOOK AT THIS IN A DIFFERENT WAY

THROUGHOUT THIS BOOK we have been working to better understand and prepare for potential long-term care needs. We have been trying to mitigate the effects that this process will have on our lives, our families, and our wealth.

I have found that most people are worried about losing what they have worked so hard to gain—usually their money and their independence.

We spend our lives making sure we have enough money, the right job, the right house, the right car, and so on. By the time we reach our elderhood, hopefully we are finding out what really matters. Perhaps old age is offering us an opportunity to shift our focus away from the physical and fleeting, toward things that never change and that cannot be taken away. As a result, material things may become less important at this stage of life.

*Perhaps together we can find a better way
to look at the concept of getting old.*

Yesterday we were businesspeople or parents. Throughout our lives we identified ourselves with what we did. As we age, we watch the conditions of our lives change. However, we are still the same people. Aging does not alter who we are inside. I remember my dad, when he turned 90, saying to me that he felt the same inside as he did when he was 25. As we are forced to slow down, we can better appreciate that part of ourselves—the part the world doesn't see on the outside. Growing old can allow us to understand our true nature and may help us to live in our aging bodies with grace rather than denial.

Perhaps together we can find a better way to look at the concept of getting old. Most of us struggle against the inevitable. We often fear the loss of our physical and mental capabilities. We fear loneliness and the loss of our contribution to society. The whole ordeal can be terribly depressing if we focus on the wrong things. Maybe we can change the way we look at this scenario.

Several months before Dad died, my 87-year-old mother was diagnosed with a condition known as progressive supranuclear palsy. It took away her ability to speak in sentences. At first, she just started repeating certain words. Then she became increasingly mute. All my life I wanted my mom to stop telling me what to do. Ironically, I now would have given anything to hear her voice again.

On July 2, 2012, the hospice nurse told me that Daddy had begun the process of dying. She couldn't tell me how long it would take, but she thought I had time to go to the office and clean things up so I could be with him and Mom at the end. He left his body a few hours later before I made it home. He left so quietly that my mom didn't know it had happened until I got home. Her cry of pain broke the rest of my heart.

Mom was fully aware that Dad had passed away, but couldn't tell me how she felt. She only cried in bed when I would come to be with her in the morning. Every day my heart broke a little more for the helplessness of the situation.

My mom was fully in that space between her former physical life and the eternal place to where we all return. As sad as it was to watch her decline, I now understand what a precious gift she gave me during our last months together. The unspoken love that we shared is our forever gift to each other. What I could not hear could be seen in her eyes. I learned how to love my mom in a whole new dimension, one we never could have experienced if we were still able to speak to each other.

I don't remember my mother rocking me, feeding me, or changing me, but she did. Is that experience any less wonderful because I don't remember it? It does not matter that my mother can't remember that I held her yesterday. How much love she felt in just that moment, I can never know; but I felt it and that meant love was there.

Her mother's love was still inside, even if she was unable to express it verbally. Looking at the situation in a different way offered me the opportunity to focus on that part of her that was most important—her soul. I could love her there. We could be together there, in that place where we recognize that we are all ageless souls in aging bodies. Mom passed away six months after Dad, but we are still connected.

What if we start the journey out of our adulthood by recognizing each other as eternally connected souls? Throughout our lives we act as if we are separate from each other, but inside we know we are all connected.

- I am that old woman sitting along the wall of the nursing home.

- I am the daughter who comes across as so disagreeable because I'm frustrated that Mom won't cooperate, but scared of losing her at the same time.

- I am the lady with Alzheimer's who used to teach me in school.

Aging—we all resist it. But sometimes the thing we resist the most bestows upon us the greatest, most unexpected blessings. As our abilities and physical life are leaving, we are offered a place for our souls to be together. We can continue to love each other in a new and deeper way, as we recognize each other on a new level.

Since they passed away, I realize that Mom and Dad are still loving me from that place we created together while I cared for them. It takes a lot of humility to move into that space, knowing

May you die young, at a very old age.
— Anonymous

Daddy sang at my wedding, June 2, 2007. He was 91.

how imperfect our attempts are to be there for each other. But we should move anyway! Even if we fail, forget, get angry, or feel sorry for ourselves, the space we create there is wide and forgiving.

As we get older, we may find ourselves increasingly dependent upon others. That dependency offers everyone a chance for great blessings. As we are forced to surrender our old ideas about who we thought we were, we may find that part of ourselves that is eternally valuable.

Remember, we are all "pearls of great value, hidden inside lovely but passing shells...."*

I may not know you, but I embrace you for caring enough about someone to have read this book. It was written with love, in the hope that we can all share a better elderhood together.

*From Father Richard Rohr in a recent meditation.

179

GLOSSARY

A

Activities of daily living (ADLs) – basic actions that independently functioning individuals perform on a daily basis: eating, bathing, dressing, transferring (moving to and from a bed or a chair), and caring for incontinence. Many public programs determine eligibility for services according to a person's need for help with ADLs.

Acute care – health treatment that requires a hospital stay. *See also "sub-acute care."*

Adult day services – structured programs that provide social and support services for the elderly in a protective setting during part of the day, but not 24-hour care.

Advance directives – documents that provide instructions to a person designated to manage the affairs of another if that person becomes unable to do so himself. A health-care proxy, living will, and power of attorney are examples of advance directives.

Agent – *see "power of attorney."*

Alzheimer's disease – progressive, degenerative form of dementia that causes severe intellectual deterioration.

Ancillary probate – probate proceeding in addition to the primary probate; often occurs when someone has property in more than one state.

Annuity – financial contract in which a consumer provides money to an insurance company that is later distributed back to the person over time; requires the designation of a beneficiary and supersedes the terms of a will. With an *immediate annuity,* the insurance company is paid up front and the consumer receives a monthly check for a specific period of time, or for the rest of his or her life.

Assisted-living facility or residence (ALF or ALR) – residential living arrangement that provides individualized personal care, assistance with activities of daily living, help with medications and services such as laundry and housekeeping; may also provide health and medical care, but care is not as intensive as that offered at a nursing home. *See also "enhanced assisted living."*

Attorney-in-fact – person who holds a power-of-attorney document that gives him or her written authorization to transact business and execute documents for another person.

B

Beneficiary – person who receives the benefits from a will or trust.

Benefit triggers – criteria used by an insurance company to determine when a beneficiary is eligible to receive benefits. For long-term care insurance, these triggers are often needing help with two or more activities of daily living or having a cognitive impairment such as Alzheimer's disease.

C

Caregiver – anyone who helps care for an elderly individual with a disability who lives at home; usually provides assistance with activities of daily living and other essential activities like shopping, meal preparation, and housework.

Caregiver agreement – contract outlining the duties and pay for caring for a family member at home; must follow strict rules to be considered valid for Medicaid coverage.

Certified Financial Planner (CFP) – designation conferred by the Certified Financial Planner Board of Standards; recipients must meet education, examination, experience, and ethics requirements set by the CFP Board.

Certified in Long-Term Care (CLTC) – independent professional certification for individuals selling long-term care insurance.

Cognitive impairment – deficiency in short- or long-term memory; orientation to person, place, and time; deductive or abstract reasoning; or judgment as it relates to safety awareness. Alzheimer's disease is an example.

Community-based services – services and service settings in the community such as adult day services, home-delivered meals, or transportation; designed to help people stay in their homes as independently as possible.

Community Medicaid Waiver programs – programs that provide home care through Medicaid (do not require a review of the recipient's gifting over the past five years).

Community spouse – someone living at home who is the spouse of a nursing-home resident applying for or receiving Medicaid long-term care services.

Comprehensive geriatric-care assessment – a multidimensional diagnostic process to determine an elderly person's medical, psychological, and functional capability; used to develop a coordinated plan for treatment and followup.

Continuing-care retirement community (CCRC) – retirement complex that offers a range of services and levels of care, typically including independent living, assisted living, and nursing-home care; residents can move to the next level as needed.

Contractual ownership *(designated-beneficiary accounts)* – assets held under the terms of a contract with a financial institution that designate a beneficiary to receive the funds upon the death of the owner; the assets transfer directly to the beneficiary, separate from the terms of the owner's will, unless the estate is named as the beneficiary of the account.

Countable assets – assets whose value is counted in determining financial eligibility for Medicaid.

Custodial care *(also called "personal care")* – non-skilled service or care, such as help with bathing, dressing, eating, getting in and out of a bed or chair, and toileting.

D

Death benefit – amount on a life insurance policy or pension payable to the beneficiary when the annuitant passes away.

Deed transfer with a retained life estate – technique allowing a property owner to give someone (often his or her children) part ownership now of a property interest that will be in place after the owner's death, when full ownership will be directly transferred without going through probate.

Deficit Reduction Act of 2005 (DRA) – law enacted to slow the growth of Medicaid, Medicare, and other government programs; it mandated stricter and more complicated rules for transferring assets to qualify for nursing-home care under Medicaid.

Dementia – deterioration of mental faculties from a brain disorder.

Disabled – for Medicaid eligibility purposes, someone whose physical or mental condition prevents him or her from doing work needed for self-support; the condition must be expected to last for at least a year or to result in death.

Discharge planner – worker who helps determine where a patient will be moved after a hospital stay, usually either to the patient's home or a rehabilitation facility.

Domicile – the location of a person's permanent home; where he or she legally resides.

Donor *(also called "grantor")* – person who creates a trust and puts assets into it.

Do Not Resuscitate Order (DNR) – written order from a doctor that resuscitation should not be attempted if a person suffers cardiac or respiratory arrest.

Durable power of attorney – legal document that gives someone the authority to act on another's behalf on specified matters. The task can be specific or broad, such as carrying out financial duties; continues through the incapacity of the individual.

E

Elimination period *(also called "deductible period" or "benefit waiting period")* – in long-term care insurance, a specified amount of time at the beginning of a disability during which covered services are received but the policy does not pay benefits.

Enhanced assisted living / assisted-living residences (ALRs) – facilities authorized to provide services that allow residents to age in place, including those who would otherwise not meet the guidelines to stay in a regular assisted-living setting; facilities with this certification can retain residents who need assistance with transferring, walking, or even nursing care. *See also "assisted living facility."*

Entitlement program – a government program guaranteeing access to some benefit. Social Security, Medicare, Medicaid, and military retirement plans are examples.

Equity value – fair-market value of property minus any liabilities on the property such as mortgages or loans. *See also "fair-market value."*

Estate – total assets of a person at the time of death.

Estate recovery – process by which Medicaid recovers an amount of money from the estate of a person who received Medicaid.

Executor – person appointed to administer the estate of someone who has died. An executor's main duty is to carry out the wishes and instructions of the deceased.

Exempt assets – *see "non-countable assets."*

F

Fair-market value – the price at which property transfers between a willing buyer and a willing seller who are both acting rationally and with complete knowledge of the situation. For Medicaid eligibility purposes, fair-market value must be received for the assets transferred under the contract. *See also "equity value."*

Fiduciary – someone entrusted to hold and manage the money of another.

Financial eligibility *(for Medicaid)* – assessment of a person's available income and assets to determine if he or she meets Medicaid eligibility requirements.

Functional eligibility *(for Medicaid)* – assessment of a person's care needs to determine whether he or she meets the Medicaid financial eligibility requirement that care is medically necessary.

G

Grantor *(also called "donor")* – person who creates a trust and puts assets into it.

Guardian – person appointed by the court to manage the affairs of a person who is legally unable to do so, especially an incompetent or disabled person or a child without parents.

H

Health-care proxy – legal document that authorizes someone to make health-care decisions for another if that person becomes unable to make or communicate those decisions for himself.

Hospice care – short-term, supportive care for individuals who have a life expectancy of six months or less; focuses on pain management and emotional, physical, and spiritual support for the patient and family.

I

Immediate annuity – *see "annuity."*

Impoverished – level of financial hardship, as defined by Medicaid, that a person must prove to be eligible for Medicaid.

Informal caregiver – any person who provides long-term care services without pay.

Instrumental activities of daily living – activities not necessary for basic functioning but necessary to live independently; may include doing light housework, preparing meals, taking medication, shopping for groceries or clothes, managing money.

Intestacy – transfer process for the assets of an individual who dies without leaving a valid will.

J

Joint tenancy by the entirety – term for assets owned by a married couple who share an undivided interest in a property during their lifetimes. Gifting or selling this property requires the consent of both parties.

Joint tenancy with rights of survivorship (JTWROS) – term for assets in which owners share an equal one-half share (moiety) during life; the surviving owner receives the property by operation of law at the death of the other joint owner. Consent of both parties is required to sell or gift the property.

Joint tenancy in common (JTIC) – term for assets in which more than one person has ownership at the same time. Any owner can transfer his interest without the consent of the other owners.

L

Last will and testament – a legal document that communicates a person's wishes about the distribution of his probate property when he dies; it must follow formalities required by the state of domicile.

Letters testamentary – documents that allow an executor to transfer assets according to the directions in a will.

Life estate – *see "deed transfer with a retained life estate."*

Living trust – *see "trust"; also called revocable trust.*

Living will – document that provides instructions to a health-care representative and medical personnel regarding someone's wishes for life-sustaining treatment if he becomes incapacitated; an example of an advance directive.

Long-term care – services and supports necessary to meet health or personal care needs over an extended period of time.

Long-term care insurance – insurance policy designed to offer financial support to pay for long-term care services.

Look-back period – 60-month period before a person's application for Medicaid payment of long-term care services. Medicaid determines if transfers of assets would disqualify the applicant from receiving benefits during that time, called the penalty period.

M

Medicaid – joint federal and state public-assistance program for financing health care for those with low incomes or very high medical bills relative to income and assets. It is the largest public payer of long-term care services.

Medicare – federal program that provides hospital and medical expense benefits for people over 65 or those meeting specific disability standards. Benefits for nursing home and home health services are limited.

Medicare Supplement Insurance – private insurance policy that covers gaps in Medicare coverage.

Minimum monthly maintenance needs allowance (MMMNA) – allowance made to the spouse of a person receiving Medicaid to avoid impoverishing the healthy spouse; each state sets its own limits.

Memory-care facility – environment designed for those whose impairment makes it unsafe for them to stay at home but who do not require the intensive care of a skilled-nursing facility; residents typically live in private or semiprivate units and have scheduled activities and programs designed to enhance memory.

N

Non-countable assets *(also called "exempt assets")* – assets whose value is not counted in determining financial eligibility for Medicaid.

Nursing home *(also called "skilled-nursing facility," "long-term care facility," or "convalescent-care facility")* – licensed facility that provides general nursing care to those who are chronically ill or unable to take care of daily living needs; typically includes administering medications, assistance with oxygen, injections, as well as occupational, speech, respiratory, and physical therapies. Usually requires the services of a licensed professional such as a nurse, doctor, or therapist.

O

Observation status – designation a hospital or doctor's office gives to a patient considered to be getting outpatient treatment; under this status, a person cannot qualify for rehabilitation services covered by Medicare.

P

Payer of last resort – term indicating Medicaid's status as payer for long-term health care after all other assets of the potential recipient have been exhausted.

Pension – regular payment from an investment fund made to a person during his retirement or to the person's surviving dependents. A worker or his employer can contribute to this fund.

Personal care – *see "custodial care."*

Pooled trust – a trust administered by a nonprofit association that pools the resources of many beneficiaries; can be used to reduce income for Community Medicaid eligibility but allow use of these funds to pay for goods and services for the beneficiary.

Power of appointment – *(example)* authority to rename the beneficiaries of a will, trust, or property; this authority can be kept by the person writing the will or trust, or given to another.

Power of attorney (*also called "agent"*) – person granted the legal power to carry out specific transactions on another's behalf, by the terms of a document such as a will.

Principal – person who appoints a power of attorney or agent to act on his or her behalf.

Probate – legal process of proving the validity of a will; governs the procedures used by an executor to complete the collection and distribution of those assets; is a public process.

R

Remainderman – person given a future interest in a property who is therefore entitled to inherit the property upon the death of the life tenant. *See "deed transfer with a retained life estate."*

Respite care – temporary care intended to provide time off for those who care for someone on a regular basis.

Revocable trust – *see "trust."*

Right of election – law by which a person can claim certain assets of a deceased spouse's estate even if the spouse willed nothing to that person; elective shares are governed by state laws, which vary.

Right of survivorship – the right of a survivor to the interest in property held in a joint tenancy upon the death of one tenant; the surviving joint tenant immediately becomes the owner of the whole property.

S

Shared-care policy – type of long-term care insurance policy for a couple that pools benefits that can be split between the spouses.

Single-ownership asset – an asset owned by one person who alone controls it and its distribution during his lifetime.

Skilled care or **skilled-nursing care** – *see "nursing home."*

Spend down – requirement that an individual spend most of his or her income and assets to pay for care before satisfying Medicaid's financial eligibility criteria.

State partnership policy – a public/private partnership between a state's department of health (Medicaid) and the insurance industry that allows the policyholder to keep some or all of his or her assets when applying for Medicaid after using up the policy's benefits. The Deficit Reduction Act of 2005 allows any state to establish a partnership program.

Supervisory care – long-term care service for people with memory or orientation problems; ensures that people don't harm themselves or others because their memory, reasoning, and orientation to person, place, or time are impaired.

Supplemental Security Income (SSI) – program administered by the Social Security Administration that provides financial assistance to needy people who are disabled or 65 or older. Many states provide Medicaid without further application to people who are eligible for SSI.

T

Trust – a legal arrangement in which a person (called a "grantor" or "donor") gives instructions regarding the distribution of assets for beneficiaries. *See "revocable" and "irrevocable" trusts, next page.*

Trust—revocable *(also called a "living trust")* – document created by an individual allowing for the separation of the legal and beneficial ownership of an asset; the trustee owns the assets and invests and maintains them, and can change the terms any time.

Trust—irrevocable – document used to remove assets from a person's ownership for various planning reasons; often established to help protect assets.

Trustee – person in charge of managing assets in a trust; makes all financial and management decisions regarding trust assets, according to the instructions written by the grantor in the trust document.

W

Will – *see "last will and testament."*

Will substitutes – various methods of transferring funds on death so that the funds transfer directly and not under the terms of a last will and testament, therefore avoiding the probate process.

Note: Definitions are to help explain terms used in this book; they are not to be used as a legal reference or to be considered a complete definition for each term.

ACKNOWLEDGMENTS

THERE ARE MANY PEOPLE I have to thank for helping me bring this book to you. I could say it starts and ends with my mom and dad, and that would be true. They sat at my bedside for three months while I was in intensive care at the age of 27, singing Dean Martin songs to me while I was in a coma. I had been Mercy-Flighted to Toronto, so they moved into a hotel and didn't leave until they brought me home. I could never love them as well as they loved me. We never quit on each other and their love sustains me even now, as they dance, together again in eternity.

My brother, William Menzies, and sister, Marilyn Peyton, walked with me through the end of our parents' lives. They taught me more than I expected about love and caring. We all have different relationships with our parents and each one is special. It takes love and understanding to handle the unexpected family stresses of helping aging parents. I am so glad we had each other then, and now, as we create a new "family," without our mom and dad.

There are people and events that have contributed to my career as an elder attorney. They include Karen Nicholson, who hired me as an intern at Legal Services for the Elderly and believed in me before I believed in myself. The lawyers I worked for in larger firms gave me the courage to step out on my own. And my mentor, David Pfalzgraf, saw something in me that I didn't see: I was a good lawyer because I cared about my clients most.

I have to thank my wonderful law partner, Chuck Beinhauer, who has been my big brother and spiritual teacher. Together, we have created a firm that has changed the lives of hundreds of elders and their families in positive ways. We have helped everyone who has crossed our doorstep in the best way we know how, and the result is a 10-year success story with the community of Western New York. Thanks go to our business coach Rick Wallace for continually pushing us toward greater service. My younger partners, Jamie Smith and Frank Vavonese, are skilled attorneys who make it a pleasure to come to work with them every day. They are better lawyers than I could ever hope to be.

My good friend and colleague, Beverly Kubala, took on the challenge to become a geriatric-care manager at our firm, and continues to teach me how to help families with kindness and compassion every day.

I work with some of the best financial professionals you will ever meet, all accomplished and comprehensive in their approach to planning, including Elizabeth Hulley, Robert Wills, and Christopher Shafer. They share their knowledge with me as we help our clients create the best financial future for their families.

And my clients—without their willingness to share their personal hopes and fears about the future, I wouldn't have such a passion to help. They become like family as we walk through their elderhood together. I learn from them every day and become a better person through the shared experience of working with them during stressful times.

I couldn't have gotten this book in proper form and would never have had half as much fun putting it together without the help of Bill Even—we'll call him my technical guru. And the graphics and copy editing have been done by Jamie Baylis, whom I have yet to meet in person! Thanks go out to my niece, Tiffany Pache, for introducing us and doing some early edits. My work-sister and marketing director, Susan Kirkpatrick, makes me look good and provides a reality check when I need one.

Finally my husband, David James, M.D., who is my chief cook, best friend, and an outstanding father to Liam and Isabella, the best dogs in the world. He makes me want to be a better person every day. I will never accomplish so much in a week as he does in one day. Besides, I had to write a book so he wasn't the only author in the house. His respect for my work helps me create miracles with each new endeavor I pursue.

To be really honest, the power of God's love in my life does all the work. I just have to show up.

About the Author

Laurie Menzies is an elder law attorney, advocate, and frequent speaker on issues related to seniors and their families, particularly regarding comprehensive planning from a legal, financial, and long-term care perspective. Having served as her parents' primary caregiver until their passing in their nineties, Laurie is personally acquainted with the struggles that seniors and their families encounter with the current fragmented and confusing long-term care system that often leaves them overwhelmed.

When they founded Pfalzgraf, Beinhauer & Menzies, Laurie and her partner created the only law firm solely dedicated to elder law and estate planning in Western New York. She is a regular writer and speaker on issues related to aging. Laurie is a graduate of Vassar College and University at Buffalo Law School. She serves on the board of directors for the Network in Aging of Western New York, WNY chapter of the Alzheimer's Association, and Canterbury Woods Continuing Care Community. Laurie has been recognized multiple times by Business First of Buffalo's Who's Who in Law.

She lives in Getzville, NY, with her husband, Dr. David James, and her dogs, Liam and Isabella.

CPSIA information can be obtained at www.ICGtesting.com
Printed in the USA
LVOW02s1739050215

425863LV00012B/19/P